More Praise for
Professional Services Marketing 3.0

Legal marketing opens the doors through which lawyers walk to develop business. Over a 60-year career in marketing, nobody has opened more of those doors, and successfully led more lawyers through, than Bruce Marcus. Now, at a critical inflection point in the profession's history, Bruce looks back to show us where we've been and looks forward to show us where we're going – the doors yet to be opened. I strongly recommend you follow him through.

> Jordan Furlong
> Law21 and Partner, Edge International

Throughout his extraordinary career, Bruce Marcus has been teaching us to grasp the fundamental unchanging truths of professional marketing even as we respond to the inevitable changes and challenges that expanding marketplaces dictate. *Professional Services Marketing 3.0* is a wise study of where we are now, how we got here, and where we need to go next. Here, simply, is the voice of a master.

> Richard S. Levick, Esq.,
> President & CEO
> Levick Strategic Communications

Who better to hold the lamp high while we struggle toward a more rational and humane future for the professions? I am reminded again of Bruce Marcus' unflagging intelligence and his extraordinary clarity and perspective on the subject of marketing knowledge services – or, to be more precise, managing the business of knowledge services. I'm grateful to find yet another of Bruce's books in my hands, giving fine shape to the future in a way that makes it seem possible.

> Merrilyn Astin Tarlton
> Attorney at Work

In *Professional Services Marketing 3.0*, Bruce Marcus has repeated and updated many of his musings from over the years. His use of historical references demonstrates both consistency and evolution – some things have changed; some things have not.

History is important for professional services marketers. It helps explain why some of our recalcitrant attorneys or accountants behave the way they do, and why it can be so hard to get things done.

But Bruce also provides hope for change. In his view, the new world of professional services marketing – 3.0 – is one where marketing is integrated into the practice, and where practitioners work in partnership with professional marketers. In his book, Bruce presents examples of forward-thinking firms, and insights into where the future might lead.

With *Professional Services Marketing 3.0*, Bruce reminds us that he "got it" long before "it" even got here.

> Sally J. Schmidt
> President, Schmidt Marketing, Inc.

Bruce Marcus has written the alpha and omega of guides to marketing professional services. His book is like a GPS for navigating all the rapidly expanding possibilities for marketing to and reaching potential clients. Drawing on decades of experience, Bruce has created a thorough and practical guide that every law firm should read and use immediately.

> Pamela Woldow
> General Counsel & Partner, Edge International, LLC.

This book is a must-read for those interested in what the future holds for professionals seeking growth in this new millennium. Timely, relevant and focused.

> Christian Payne
> CEO, Kellogg & Andelson CPAs

Bruce Marcus has been pushing back the frontiers of legal marketing since its very start, and now he is at it again. His new book not only provides a picture of where legal marketing is now, it also explains where it is going next. Don't miss this definitive guide to where legal marketing is going, from a thought leader who's been charting its course since the very beginning.

> Jim Hassett
> Founder, LegalBizDev

If you're breathing, you're marketing. Not everyone realizes this truth, but great rainmakers and those who are looking to thrive in the New Normal certainly do. You can choose to ignore this truth and suffer the inevitable consequences, or you can study the wisdom shared by Bruce Marcus in *Professional Services Marketing 3.0*, implement what you learn and be among those who thrive in this ever changing world. You can hang on and pray or choose to steer the ship intelligently. Those who read Bruce's latest book will be in the latter group.

> Patrick Lamb
> Founding Member, Valorem Law Group

Bruce Marcus has the uncanny ability to take a hot-button topic and soothingly – but incisively – cut to the heart of the matter: Everything you think you know about marketing has changed. In a fast-paced, wonderfully written look at marketing today and in the future, Marcus shows the reader how enormously this field has changed in a few short decades – and how it is changing now. Law firm marketing professionals and attorneys alike should use this book as their bible.

> Wendy Ampolsk Stavinoha
> Senior Legal and Marketing Editor

This is so much more than just a marketing book for professionals. Instead, Bruce Marcus has crafted a manifesto for the coming revolution that will forever change how professionals serve their clients. With his decades of real-world experience and wisdom, Bruce Marcus is the perfect guide for navigating this change. If you're a professional – even one who hates the idea of marketing – and you want to better reach and serve clients, you must read *Professional Services Marketing 3.0.*

> Jay Shepherd
> CEO of Prefix, LLC
> Author of *TheClientRevolution.com*

Bruce Marcus has once again knocked it out of the park! *Professional Services Marketing 3.0* will be the bible for business developers and marketing savvy lawyers and accountant and their support teams. Bruce Marcus teaches people to be innovative thinkers and how to successfully implement cutting edge innovations for success in business, which ultimately results in revenue generation and total client satisfaction.

> Iris Jones
> Lawyer, business development coach and trainer,
> CEO, Alchemy Business Strategies, LLC.

Lawyers and accountants, from students and novices to the most experienced professionals, can benefit from Bruce Marcus, a marketing guru who, for decades, has helped lawyers, accountants and other professionals to communicate more effectively. In fact, his new book is so delightfully written that anyone in banking and related fields, as well as people in advertising, public relations, sales and other areas of marketing, can enjoy and benefit by reading it.

> Richard Weiner
> Author of 23 books about public relations and media

Professional Services Marketing 3.0 is a key guide for anyone working in the professions. It is more than part "The Essential Marcus" -an anthology of the author's best articles spanning 5-plus decades and part a chronicle of the development of marketing in the professions: charmingly mixed with autobiographical elements, Marcus challenges conventional wisdom and looks at what's yet to come, and yet to be done. In a time of increased competition, lawyers, accountants and their marketers have to work closer together than ever, and use smarter, rather than merely more marketing. Marcus' book should appeal to newcomers to accounting and law firm marketing, those needing a refresher course on best practice as well as to seasoned marketers interested in questioning the viability and effectiveness of their marketing.

> Dr. Silvia Hodges
> Fordham Law School

Bruce W. Marcus has always been the type of gentleman to get us to think. With *Professional Services Marketing 3.0*, he continues to challenge us in the ever-changing professional services marketing world. Thank you, Bruce, for sharing your wisdom and perspective on a profession we both love.

> Jean Marie Caragher
> President, Capstone Marketing

Professional Services Marketing 3.0

Bruce W. Marcus

Published by Bay Street Group LLC

For more on our other products and services, please visit http://www.baystreetgroup.com
for contact information.

Library Data
Marcus, Bruce W.
Professional Services Marketing 3.0
Bruce W. Marcus

ISBN 978-0-9827147-1-3

1. Accounting firms – Marketing. 2. Law firms – Marketing. 3. Accounting firms – United
States – Marketing. 4. Law firms – United States – Marketing

I. Marcus, Bruce W., 1925-

To My Wife, Mana

Bruce W. Marcus

Bruce W. Marcus is a pioneer in the modern practices of professional services marketing.

Following his graduation in 1951 (with a degree in Economics and Philosophy), he joined the then-Big Eight accounting firm, Peat Marwick Mitchell to establish the firm's library. Within the constraints of the ethical constrictions against promotional activities that then existed, he developed an article writing and seminar program that successfully promoted the firm's reputation. Subsequently, he served as a public relations and marketing executive or consultant to most of the international accounting firms, and many large and small law firms. His book, *Competing for Clients* (1986) was one of the first to delineate the new practices of professional services marketing, followed by more than a dozen books on professional services marketing, real estate marketing, investor relations, and international accounting standards. His first newsletter, *The Marcus Report* (1986), was followed by *The Marcus Letter* (1991) in hard copy, and then by the award-winning *www.marcusletter. com* in 1995 – one of the longest running letters on marketing for lawyers and accountants still in existence. He is on the editorial boards of several leading professional services publications, a contributor to many publications, and has been a keynote speaker at several major conferences. He taught one of the first courses in professional services marketing at the Fordham University Graduate School of Business, and lectures frequently at the Fordham University law School.

His career in marketing followed a long career in award winning public relations, as radio and television dramatist, and as a playwright and director for both Broadway, off-Broadway, and community theater.

Contents

CONTENTS

Foreword

When I first heard the title of Bruce Marcus' latest book, I thought, "Professional Services Marketing 3.0? Well, forgive me, but I think I need to be clued in on what exactly were 1.0 and 2.0." Not only does Bruce answer this question, he provides an expansive and ambitious vision of what he sees ahead for us as we cross the threshold.

Now, if you need the same help I did in recognizing 1.0 and 2.0, the first was in the wake of the 1977 U. S. Supreme Court decision in *Bates v. State Bar of Arizona*, which is commonly seen as a narrow decision striking down the prohibition on attorney advertising, but which Bruce Marcus insightfully identifies as something far more momentous: The beginning of open competition in professional services.

The second stage is where we are today, with a frank recognition of the necessity of marketing, but a time (the present) when it's still tainted by the mild whiff of the promotional, the sales-y, and the unprofessional. Bruce writes that "if there's one thing that has inhibited innovation and growth in professional services marketing in the decades since *Bates*, it's the disconnect between marketers and the professionals they serve," but I would say it goes even further. Marketers are often treated as the obligatory but unwelcome guests at the dinner party.

The problem with professional services marketing in such an environment is it doesn't work without the full engagement and participation of the professionals. (You can market a Snickers bar or a Chevy Volt or Budweiser without showcasing anyone involved in bringing them to market, but not so in our world.) And if those who must be engaged and must participate would prefer not to, the efforts stop in their tracks. Or, and this could conceivably be worse, are profoundly unconvincing and even alienating to clients.

So where does Marketing 3.0 begin?

Simply put, with the suddenly rapid evolution of our profession into The New Normal. The New Normal is not a blip after the great recession of 2007–

2009. (Yes, there are those who believe that, and part of me wishes I could come back in another life as them; it would be so much simpler.) Rather, the great recession accelerated trends and strengthened forces that had been latent and rumbling underground for years, even decades, and which have now taken firm hold.

Among those new realities are:

- Serious and meaningful price pressure from clients. Before they had threatened, now they mean it.

- A multiplying efflorescence of career paths. No longer will we be limited to the Manichean up or out of associate or partner. Yes, part of this change is ugly, as partners become de-equitized, but much provides increased humanity and flexibility, including staff, contract, and non-partner-track paths, and other forms and varieties yet to be invented or defined.

- A brand-new commitment to project management, providing clients with more price certainty.

- Smarter, data-driven recruiting practices, increasing the odds of a good match between firms and young associates, based on the real track records of people with specific behavioral profiles.

- A renewed and lifelong commitment to professional development. And most important, from the perspective of clients, sensitive, discriminating, and truly strategic structuring of firms in terms of practice area and geographic focus to tailor their offerings to what clients most value that particular firm for.

A tall order?

Indeed.

But make no mistake: Change is coming, whether the incumbents like it or not.

This is the way markets work. Their Darwinian logic mandates that when clients seek change and a competitor – almost any capable and credible competitor – responds, you will soon find your firm reacting.

The Managing Partner of an AmLaw 20 firm, who I count a friend, has observed that "ours is a very mature profession, but a very immature industry." How right he is. Among other components of that immaturity are that law firms typically have no retained earnings, making long-term capital investments forbidding and expensive to current equity partners, and that they have no way of offering an ownership stake to non-lawyers. Both these capabilities have long since been taken for granted in the corporate world.

Another difference between our world and corporate land is how we perceive the client. Peter Drucker used to like to stump business school students by posing the question, "What is *the one thing* every firm must have to exist?" The answer, of course, he would only reveal after students floundered a bit, which is "Clients." Every successful corporation knows that, but most professional service firms believe the core of their business revolves not around clients but around the professionals themselves. Professional service firms, as it were, tend to "sell what we make," whereas corporations largely "make what we sell."

The book you are holding points in the direction of changing that – and changing far, far more.

Is this, then, Professional Services Marketing 3.0? This book is actually larger than that, if you read it rightly and see it as a history pointing the way towards the future.

It strikes me it's Professional Services 3.0. Let the conversation begin.

Bruce MacEwen
Adam Smith, Esq.
New York City
March 2011

Introduction

Bruce Marcus' newest book documents an important evolution in professional firms and the way law and accounting firms interact with current and prospective buyers. These interactions include serving the client, but also – quite importantly – reflecting how people working in firms present themselves in terms of their ability to bring true value to those who hire them.

The author's approach is two-fold: understand the past, and be intentional about the future. As you read, and consider your firm's present marketing in light of this broader, historic context, you have the opportunity to identify counter-productive attitudes and approaches and move to an advanced level of marketing sooner than you otherwise might. The author shares, through his rich observations and experiences, that the views a professional holds about the value of his or her offerings, and marketing in general, are more important than the specific marketing tactics he or she undertakes.

The three phases of marketing Bruce Marcus adeptly identifies and describes (Marketing 1.0, 2.0 and 3.0) may seem linear but they most certainly overlap. While some of today's firms are well into Marketing 3.0, others are still in the Marketing 1.0 phase. There are still a few firms that have not yet entered 1.0 (a bit scary). It's even possible to have different people within a firm acting within different phases. It is difficult for a firm to progress in an environment where some minds are in an advanced phase, and others are not – and yet they have equal say – the common denominator is never the most advanced approach. This is a problem, inherent in partnerships, that is resolved with a more corporate-like operational model, for which the author also makes an excellent case.

In the mid-late 1990s, my career was in the still-young field of professional firm marketing. Accounting and law firms were both very much cutting their teeth in marketing, even a full decade after the *Bates v. State Bar of Arizona* decision. It was amid Marketing 1.0.

As the first full-time marketing director in a mid-sized, local CPA firm and then in a large, regional law firm, a too-common scenario was bringing a sound recommendation to the table and having a room full of partners squelch the concept or modify it to such an extent that it no longer resembled itself. Unfortunately, the potential effectiveness of the resulting approach was dramatically impacted through this process. I wasn't alone. Disturbing patterns began emerging in this new "professional firm marketer" field.

Knowledgeable marketing professionals gathered at their annual peer conventions (Legal Marketing Association and Association for Accounting Marketing) sharing stories of nobly fighting for their ideas. Initially. It's simply human nature that weariness of uphill battles (and being shot down) leads people to reducing their attempts at offering innovative, new ideas. Few were the marketers who forged ahead and thrived and in this environment; a very small number of veteran marketers became non-practicing owners of their firms. A far greater number of marketers fled these marketing-hostile cultures resulting in law and accounting having some of the highest attrition rates among marketing professionals across all sectors – the average tenure was between one and two years.

Other marketers stayed, keeping peace by adapting their roles to primarily that of implementer of partner-initiated or partner-approved ideas, many of which were borrowed from other firms: copycat marketing. Exacerbating the problem of originality in marketing was the requirement of partners for "evidence" or precedent of success of a marketing concept before being willing to support it. Marketing successes in this scenario were generally limited by their very nature – held to an artificial maximum – a key problem being lack of differentiation because firms were basically doing the same things as other firms.

By the time firms were on to their second or third marketing professionals, they tended to be convinced that the advice of their marketers merited greater receptiveness – that a collaborative approach between marketer and practitioners is optimal. And they began to realize, as Bruce Marcus describes, that the tools and skills of marketing are not so important as the experience and imagination of the marketer – he urges firms to value the "artist" over the "mechanic" for your marketing. He reinforces that "the tools of marketing are not a program – they are simply tools." These realizations are a large part of what lead a firm to the level of Marketing 3.0.

The author explains why competing in today's environment necessitates a *client-driven*, rather than *practice-driven* firm and that immersion in the customer's business – why quality of service is a mere table stake. He takes on "the brochure," image, and branding – discussing that reputation is reliant on performance, the intangibles, not logos and brand promises that go unmet. He teaches us that when we focus overly on enhancing our image, "we absolve ourselves of the need to nurture reputation and perception by improving reality," for marketing is irrelevant if good customers are slipping out the back door while firms spend their energy chasing new business.

The future of marketing is enhanced by understanding the past and present. It's extremely rare to meet and learn from someone with the vast experiences of Mr. Marcus. It's rarer yet to come upon a person who also maintains an extraordinarily open mind to new perspectives on the art and science of which he is already a master many times over. To study the lessons within this book is an investment well worth making; may your mind be as open as the author's as you explore the pages that follow.

Michelle Golden
St. Louis, MO
March 2011

Preface

Professional Services Marketing 3.0? This from someone who has written, spoken, railed against jargon and gimmicks?

Well, yes, because in this rapidly changing economic environment, intensely competitive landscape, and highly charged computer age, it's the best way to define significant evolution from one distinct period to the next. As you'll see in the following pages, that's exactly what's happened – and is happening – in law and accounting firm marketing. And in firm practices, business models, and structure as well.

The first stage of course – *Professional Services Marketing 1.0* – was the U.S. Supreme Court's decision in *Bates v. State Bar of Arizona*, which, in 1977, struck down the long standing and traditional Codes of Ethics and Rules of Professional Conduct that prohibited what we now call frank marketing, or any form of promotion or commercialization. In one stroke, it wiped out the many generations of practice development achieved almost solely by social contact. The word *compete* was considered an obscenity. But competition, and all that it entails, turned out to be at the heart of *Bates*. The ability to compete, using as a foundation traditional techniques of marketing, ultimately and significantly altered the nature of the legal and accounting firm practices. It began a course of evolution that brought us to the modern firms we see today. In other words, it brought meaningful change beyond the decision itself.

Marketing 2.0 is the period – we're still in it – in which the techniques of professional services marketing have been somewhat refined, and in which marketing has begun to evolve into a common practice now accepted by most once-reluctant lawyers and accountants. These techniques were not originally in the arsenal of most accounting or law firms, and for most lawyers, accountants, and their marketers the new techniques had to be learned. What was hardest to learn, it seems, was that the traditional practices and techniques used in product marketing had little currency in professional services marketing – and new techniques, predicated on the distinctive qualities of professional services, had to be developed. The professionals, to whom anything in their practices other than law or accounting was anathema, long fought against accepting the professionalism of the new marketing practitioners. "Marketing?" they would say in those early days, "Yeah, we've got a girl down the hall who does that." There are still, unfortunately, those who have yet to accept marketing as integral to practice management. Professional services marketers, in those early days, had to spend an inordinate amount of their time selling marketing to the firm's lawyers or accountants. Marketing was defined by the professionals in those days by its mythology. *"Public relations? That's free advertising, isn't it?"* No, it isn't.

If there's one thing that has inhibited innovation and growth in professional services marketing in the decades since *Bates*, it's the disconnect between marketers and the professionals they serve. While too many marketers are content to accept that disconnect, and practice their craft virtually by rote, others fight back – and sometimes win.

But that negative attitude seems to be changing, at least because since *Bates*, and the days of the lawyers and accountants who consistently spoke and thought of marketing as some kind of alien practices that they want no part of, are dwindling. A new generation of professionals has grown into positions of authority in the firms. These are lawyers and accountants who understand that marketing is as integral to a practice as are law and accounting libraries and cash flow management. This new breed of professionals understands that the environment in which they practice is tempered by competition, and that fighting competition isn't accomplished casually. There are the innovative lawyers and accountants, like Jay Shepherd and his firm, Shepherd Law Group, Patrick Lamb and his firm, Valorem, Christopher Marston's Exemplar Law Partners, and Mark Harris's Axiom Legal, for example, who rebuild or start law firms in the context of this new economic era. There are Christian Payne's remarkably innovate innovative CPA firm and the contemporary firm Seiler LLP in California.

(In a work like this, incidentally, the question sometimes arises about whether the book is for lawyers or for accountants. In fact, it's for both, as have been all my books addressing professional services marketing. I have long known that the basic tenets of professional services marketing apply almost equally to all professional services. The particular grist for the marketing mills of lawyers or accountants may offer specifics unique to each profession, but the basic principles apply equally to both. This subject is fully addressed in Chapter 6.)

An interesting characteristic about professional services marketing is that it can only be done with the full participation of the lawyers or the accountants. Not true, though, in product marketing. The professionals must supply the grist for the marketing mills. The auto and cereal companies don't have to rely on the people on the line to market. The problem with that is that when every marketing idea is a hard sell within a law or accounting firm, when every partner has something to say and says it, a lot of marketing ideas don't get into play. The lawyers and accountants had trouble understanding that they must be as conversant in marketing practice as the marketing professionals, and that marketing professionals must be substantially conversant in professional firm management That's what *Marketing 2.0* has been like, and is only now beginning to change. And here we begin to see the beginning of a new era – *Professional Services Marketing 3.0*.

But evolution often has a life of its own, and what should be is often what will be. With new generations of professionals moving into positions of authority – professionals not totally imbued with, nor inhibited by, the traditions of their elders. What is emerging, then, is *Marketing 3.0*. It is the next stage of the evolution, and while its seeds are in the past three decades since *Bates*, it portends substantial change for both the marketers and the professionals. This, I might add, is not conjecture, but demonstrable fact.

Professional Services Marketing 3.0 brings us the lawyer and accountant who is now completely conversant with the role of marketing in the practice, the techniques of marketing, and the role of the professional marketer. Where, under 2.0, it was the professional versus the marketer, we now begin to see the professional/marketer – in a new partnership.

What we see, also, are new kinds of firms, with new configurations, developed to improve productivity and client service. We see new attitudes by the professionals, and new professional-marketer relationships. It's a new step in the evolutionary process.

That's what this book is about – how to learn to swim to shore in a churning and turbulent sea of evolution and change. How to recognize and participate profitably in the incoming tide. How to use your own resources to survive and thrive when your competitors are drowning in a sea of despair. How to find and sow the seeds of opportunity in the midst of crisis. How to survive as the future unfolds.

Truth told, for all that we do know, there's still a lot of mystery about professional services marketing that we don't fathom. There's a lot of talking and writing until you get to actually selling a service – a lot of arrows shot into the air in the hope that some will land where you want them. A lot of energy, effort, and yes, money expended, in the attempt to persuade prospective clients to choose your firm rather than another – when that need for your services arises. My fond hope is that the contents of the following pages will help demystify the process.

What's different about this book is that it isn't an A to Z primer. Rather, it's a selection of my writings on professional services marketing since 1980 and before. In other words, from start to now, to a possible – *possible* – future. It draws heavily from my experience as a professional services marketer by including a selection of my writing from both *The Marcus Letter* and other publications – material of universal substance that will stand the practitioners in good stead under most conditions in both the present and the future. Some of the articles appeared, either as reprints or originally, in such publications (both online and in hard copy) as *Rain Today, Law Firm Partnership and Benefits Report, Of Counsel,* and *Law Journal Newsletter's Legal Tech Newsletter.*

It's in two sections – Section One addresses the anatomy of professional services marketing – its roots and evolutionary movement. These are the underlying elements that best define the nature and practice of contemporary professional services marketing. It describes, as well, the dynamic that drives the evolution from Marketing 1.0 to Marketing 3.0.

In Section Two are the timeless basics – the mechanics of marketing – those practices that I first defined in 1980 and subsequently, and that continue to be the practices underlying the marketing process. These chapters are also the embellishments – the refinements of the basic practices, as dictated by experience (both mine, and that of others) and evolution, and that lead to the future.

If there is any coherent theme, it's that professional services marketing is indeed an evolutionary process – starting from *Bates* as a base, and still evolving, and those factors that portend the future. In other words, adventures in the evolving anatomy of professional services marketing.

As for the future, I'm against prognostication, simply because it's impossible to do with sufficient accuracy to make it worth the effort. (See Chapter 5) Most change – as I've written before and in the following pages – is not an event, it's a process that is constantly assaulted by random and unpredictable events. Yes, there's the occasional innovator, but it's most likely to be someone who has the ability to see and respond rapidly to changing conditions in the marketplace. It's a dramatic evolution from the past three decades since *Bates*. Usually it's propelled by external forces, such as the economy, changing client needs, and technology. You can prepare for change to a degree by watching trends, and by understanding that it happens due to external forces. But unless you're a gambler, don't bet too heavily on any prediction you make for the future of your firm.

At the same time, you can extrapolate a great deal from the past and make reasonable assumptions about how the past may dictate the future. Sometimes. Not always. That's why this book draws heavily on articles I've written and speeches I've given that defined the marketing process in terms of those verities of the past that are possibly to be the verities of the future. This is simply because they have been proven to be not only workable, and ultimately to be the foundations of contemporary marketing – but also because they are likely to be as important to marketing now and in the future as they were decades ago. Some practices are immutable, not likely to change, nor should they. Some, particularly those driven by new technology, will and should change. Some changes are as complex and unpredictable as was the advent of the social media. An example is some of the stuff in the article I wrote in 1980 for *The Virginia Accountant*, which is included as Chapter 9 in the following pages. Much has changed in the interim, but they are, for the most part, embellishments. The basic verities still preside.

To understand the foundation for professional services marketing, its anatomy – as compared to that of product management and marketing – must be understood. It's at the core of professional services marketing.

There is, primarily, the difference between the structures of professional firms and those of manufacturing companies. Manufacturers have management flexibility not traditionally available to professional firms. Lawyers and accountants are constrained by the limits of partnership and the Canons of Ethics and Code of Professional Conduct that inhibit more than they allow in dealing with the public.

Manufacturers can generally acquire and allocate capital more freely and creatively than professional firms, which have limited access to capital beyond revenues and partner contributions. Too often, every partner has a say in how capital is used, and is often constrained by realizing that every penny spent comes out of his or her pocket. There is, of course, debt, but that can be an unreliable option. Obviously, ways must be found to acquire capital and use it more effectively, as well as to raise capital from external sources without jeopardizing the basic tenets of professionalism. It can be done, and at this writing, some firms are seriously considering it, particularly in Great Britain.

Manufacturing companies are usually run by managers who have either been specifically trained in management techniques, or who have acquired management skills as they moved up the corporate ladder. Lawyers are trained in law and accountants are trained in accounting. Even those professionals with MBAs have little management experience until they rise to the top of the partnership. Inherent in the training of management is the enhanced understanding of customer needs, and serving those needs – an understanding that often seems inimical to professionals.

Manufacturers know that at the core of their businesses (according to the legendary consultant, Peter Drucker) are the customers, and therefore that marketing – making and keeping new customers – is at the core of their existence. Many lawyers and accountants have yet, for the most part, to grasp this concept, and to know that marketing is integral to their success. Professionals too frequently see marketing as ancillary to the practice. Necessity now requires that activities be measured in terms of the needs of our times – of the economy, of technology, of the changing demands of the clientele, and certainly of competition.

Manufacturers can change virtually on a moment's notice to adapt to competition, to changing public needs and tastes, or to technological advances. Professionals, bound by traditions and the rules of each profession's practices and professional societies, as well as an inflated sense of their own value, tend to equate change with devil worship – or at least as a threat to the integrity of the practice. Considering these distractions, and the ways in which they inhibit professional firms, think of what marvelous opportunities exist for the venturesome lawyer and the imaginative accountants – often by overcoming traditional obstacles. The future, I believe, lies in recognizing these differences, and understanding that much in this venue must be made more relevant to the needs of the current and emerging economic, social and technical environment. In other words, the practices of law and accounting can't continue to function in the new competitive environment as they have for so many generations.

Let me here reiterate another basic point about this book. When I talk about process or technique, none of it's academic theory. Everything I write or otherwise advocate is something I've tested and done, and know from firsthand experience actually works.

The first book I wrote on professional services marketing, in the early 1980s, was called *Competing for Clients*. It led to the hard copy newsletter, *The Marcus Report*, which then became *The Marcus Letter*, which then became www.marcusletter.com. I know that much of what I did in those early days – I had an accounting firm marketing client prior to *Bates*, so I guess that makes me a pioneer – had never been done before by lawyers or accountants. Some of it was adapted from product marketing, because we learned early on that professional services marketing was very different from product marketing, and there were no predecessors to teach us how to deal with those differences. Until we got it right, we made mistakes, and ideas and techniques had to be either adapted or rejected, but we learned. And what we learned always wound up in writing. These ideas and concepts were honed in work I did for many accounting and law firms, both large and small. Not in a vacuum, though. I know some very smart people.

I've always had help from good friends whose major assets, for me, were that they were smarter than I am. Long list, but readers and other marketing professionals will know most of them. Gerry Riskin, Patrick McKenna, Larry Smith, Bruce MacEwen, Janet Stanton, Sally Schmidt, Silvia Coulter, Suzanne Lowe, Louise Rothery, Michelle Golden, Jordan Furlong, Ron Baker, Jay Shepherd, Gale Crosley, ALM's Wendy Kaplan Stavinhoa and Steve Salkin, Richard Levick, Peter Horowitz, Silvia Hodges, Jean Caragher, Accounting Today's excellent editor, Bill Carlino, and Ken Wright stand out, among many others. My friend and publisher, Rick Telberg, was the best trade book editor I ever knew, and knows more about the accounting profession than most accountants. David Maister, a fellow pioneer and an insightful consultant to the professions, has on many occasions been the wind beneath my wings. His one-firm firm concept is a goal for every firm to aspire to. Richard Chaplin, founder and CEO of England and Europe's Practice Management International LLP, and publisher of *PM, Professional Marketing* magazine, and its brilliant editor, Nadia Cristina, are long time friends and hosts , as well as publisher of many of my articles. Mine own accountant, Karen Giammattei, has been a valuable resource. I owe a lot to my first real mentor, Dick Weiner, who, when he hired me at Ruder & Finn in 1959, taught me how to think like a marketer and how to listen to clients, and whose strongest virtue as a teacher, in addition to his uncanny imaginative and lightning mind, may have been his patience with my youthful enthusiasm. Mike Giglio, a master of project management, helped me put it into perspective. And without the technical help of my good friend (and former Microsoft tech support genius), Brett Schuhmacher, I'd still be writing by pen and ink. David Urbanik, Chief Operating Officer of Halloran & Sage, LLP, who inspired the concept of Marketing 3.0 by virtue of being a prime example of the new marketing-oriented law firm professional, triggers my thinking about the whole subject of professional services marketing. And as I write this, my former boss at Ruder and Finn, Bill Ruder, has just passed away. A unique and powerful innovator in the public relations field, I learned a great deal about selling and client relations from him. He was both brilliant and warm. And more than most, he helped bring maturity to the public relations field.

I know it's traditional for authors to thank wives in a book. But my wife,

Mana, specifically and actively encouraged me during the task of writing this and many other books. For the many years of our marriage, and the many books and articles I've written and continue to write, she has personified the wisdom and intelligence that fuels an author's efforts. She is one very smart lady. She reads my stuff and guards me against saying foolish things. For this, I thank her profusely.

My first job in the professions in 1951 was for the accounting firm that was then called Peat, Marwick, Mitchell. It was a revelation to a young man, fresh out of the World War II Army Air Force, with a background in the theater and a degree in economics and philosophy. I had worked my way through college after the war as a clerk in the business reference division of the Brooklyn Public Library. Peat Marwick had just merged with another accounting firm, and I was retained in 1951 to integrate the libraries and serve as the librarian. The firm, back then, and the profession, were run pretty much as they had been when Mr. Peat met Mr. Marwick somewhere around the turn of the 20th century.

Among the many things I learned in that job, in addition to the a lot about the accounting profession, were the Canons of Ethics and the Code of Professional Conduct that prohibited frank marketing (as opposed to what might be called social contact practice development) as we know it today. Because part of my Air Force work after the Japanese surrender entailed a measure of public relations, I suggested to the accountants that because educating clients was a normal responsibility, doing so on a planned basis might be a good way to enhance practice development. To a limited degree, the accountants accepted this, and a few other ideas, such as the judicious use of articles in client trade journals. And there went virtue.

Subsequently, working with accounting and law firms of all sizes gave me not only similar insights into those professions, but gave me to understand the differences in marketing techniques – slight as they were – between law and accounting firms. The similarities, however, are not only in marketing techniques, but it in the professionals' attitudes toward marketing generally.

I mention this because most of this book is about where we were then, where we went afterwards, where we are now, and where we may be going next. Or more accurately, what kind of future we may be entering now.

It's also about what hasn't changed in professional service marketing that should have. Thus, included is the article I wrote on accounting firm marketing in 1980 (Chapter One) that's as accurate and effective today as it was then – despite the vast changes that have taken place in the professions, in the economy, in business, since then. As the noted scientist, Stephen Jay Gould, reminded us, evolution can be a slow process.

Some of the marketing practices I wrote about in the 1970s and 1980s are still relevant today – some because they're still useful, (like public relations, which hasn't changed much in decades, except for the ingenuity of some of those who practice it). Some are relevant but not as useful as they could be (like advertising) because the message hasn't penetrated to Madison Avenue. There's also the fact that new people keep coming into the field as beginners, and have much to learn about basics.

Set forth in the following pages are ideas and suggestions for a rational approach to finding and seizing opportunities for growth in a time when others are retrenching.

These proposals and ideas are not, as they say in the pharmaceutical industry, for everyone. They are not for the hidebound, the tradition bound, nor the unimaginative professional who thinks that the long-standing traditions of professional practice will revive and save the day. They require boldness, vision, and management skills. Then they work.

I once got into an argument with a partner in one of the then-Big Eight accounting firms about an ad we were doing. Finally, in exasperation, he said to me, "Look – I have a degree in finance and accounting and an MBA. I had to pass a tough test to get my CPA, and served a decade-long apprenticeship to become a partner. And I say we do it my way."

To which I replied, "What we do in marketing isn't exactly nuclear physics. But we have our training, our skills, and our experience. And I say we must do it my way." And we did.

In many firms today, that story is anachronistic. And that's the future of law and accounting firm marketing. Read on to see why.

Branford, CT
March 2011

[Section One]

The Anatomy Of
Professional Services Marketing

The concepts, ideas, history, and future
that inherently define and drive
professional services marketing
– past, present, and especially, future –
from Marketing 1.0 to Marketing 3.0

{Chapter 1}

Professional Services Marketing 3.0

How We Got From Marketing 2.0 To Here

Recently, I've been rereading the works of the late lawyer and novelist Louis Auchincloss, who wrote so meticulously and vibrantly about life in the legal and social world in the early and mid-20th Century. The legal profession was rigid and class-defined, a caste system governed by strict ethical rules, a hierarchical structure with great distance between the levels of a firm from managing partner to the lowest clerks (whom we now call associates), and by both money and status in society. To preserve the integrity and probity of the profession, there was an aloofness – an elitism – that set lawyers apart from the rest of the working world.

In 1951, when I joined the then-Big Eight accounting firm Peat, Marwick, Mitchell as its librarian, accounting firms were virtually identical to law firms in their elitism and attitude. In the offices of both professions, there were no first names in the ranks above and below one's own status, women were never called by their first names, and jackets and ties for the men and dresses and stockings for the women (most of whom were secretaries or clerks) were obligatory. Client development was done primarily by networking in social venues, such as country clubs, golf courses, and in politics, and by client referrals. The commercial aspect of professional services was rarely discussed in public. I had been a journalist, and had done some public relations in the Air Force during World War II. When I suggested that there might be ways to develop the practice within the bounds of the AICPA's Code of Professional Conduct other than the traditional social contact methods then used, many of the partners were horrified (but they did it anyway.) If the word competition was heard in the corridors of those firms, it usually referred to squash or tennis – certainly not to the legal or accounting professions.

No brochures, no press releases, no client retention plans, no direct mail nor any form of advertising (except new partner announcements) no knowledge management, no marketers, no active concern about value, no horrible jargon like rainmakers or branding or niche marketing.

In both professions, such concepts as cross selling rarely existed, because each partner felt that his clients were his first, and then the firm's. We often heard such expressions as "I love you Charlie – you're my partner and my friend – but stay away from my clients."

Clients were much less sophisticated than they are today, and most often unquestioning about advice. Very little attempt was made in either profession to educate them beyond the matters at hand. This aloofness, I think, was designed to maintain the aura of superiority of the all-knowing professional. The firm, not the client, was at the core of the practice. It was the firm, as much or more than the client, that defined the problem or matter and cast the solution. And all this was true for both professions.

Notes David Urbanik, long an outstanding law firm manager, "30 years ago the primary decision factor to retain a lawyer was the perceived specific skills of the lawyer. Today, a greater and greater percentage of legal work once thought of as complex is considered to be commodity work for which the supply of lawyers judged to be competent to do the work is large. Much of it is outsourced, both domestically and abroad. At the same time, clients are putting much greater value on how the service is delivered."

Says Pamela Woldow, an attorney with the prestigious international consulting firm Edge International, "Most commentators agree that the economically-driven sea change in the legal profession has changed the way legal services are procured and has shifted the balance of negotiating and pricing power from law firms to their clients. Corporate counsel now have mandates from the C-Suite to do more with less, contain costs, think outside the box and be smarter in how they use and manage outside counsel."

Moreover, says Woldow, "The language of many current RFPs now includes very specific questions not just about a firm's legal expertise, but about how legal services will be delivered, budgeted, monitored and managed. In-house counsel are making clear what they want to pay and how they want services delivered. Increasingly, they also have begun to insist that their outside law firms provide additional no-cost perks."

To which Michelle Golden, one of the most experienced of the accounting firm consultants, adds, "Today, more than at any time in the past three decades, practice specialization holds the key to de-commoditizing professional firm knowledge offerings. And focusing on the fact that the true value in what firms deliver comes from 'knowledge' versus 'service' is at the core of effective positioning and much needed price improvement. We're moving toward the need for business model changes that move firms 100% towards client-centricity in all functional area."

How did we get from the neo-Dickensian practices of those early days to today's modern firm? How did we evolve into the focus on competition and business development, on management science, on value billing and two-tier structures, on the serious practice of managing a firm's knowledge in many areas, on forming virtual partnerships with clients, or client service teams, and even on office informality?

The need to understand this process is more than an intellectual exercise. It's a guide to understanding where we really are, and how to function better in this new environment. It's a blueprint for functioning better within the context of today's economic, social, and technological environment. Understanding the process of evolution – yes, evolution – that produces meaningful change better informs us on how to compete more effectively, as well as to anticipate and prepare for the future progress of this evolution. It enhances the validity and simplifies the process of long-range planning.

The Contemporary Firm

Today's modern firm – and there are more of them than we think, and fewer of them than we'd like to think – is still evolving. Change, as we shall see in the next chapter, is the result of an evolutionary process – and evolution in a dynamic world is an imperative, and ongoing.

Today's modern firm is sufficiently different from those of the last century as to be almost unrecognizable to the old timers. It tends to be more client oriented. It's informal in internal and external relationships, and appropriately formal when the legal or accounting practices demand it. New concepts of governance are beginning to emerge – even to the point of considering the publicly held professional firm. Both accounting and law firms increasingly speak of a concept called value – what is the value to the clients of the knowledge and skills we provide? – which puts greater pressure on the traditional and somewhat archaic hourly valuation of client service. In many firms, hourly pricing is being replaced with the more substantive value pricing, based on the value of the matter to the client.

While the structure and business models of accounting firms differ in several significant and obvious, ways from those of law firms, the contemporary environment for both professions have much in common. For example, both professions face a changing relationship with clients. For both, the era of the somewhat docile client is vanishing, thus affecting the ways in which each profession must function in the marketplace. At the same time, both professions are experiencing commoditization of traditional legal and accounting practices, which, in today's electronic environment, readily facilitates outsourcing to highly qualified lawyers and accountants in such countries as India, the Philippines and even China.

To have dreamed of outsourcing legal or accounting processes to a foreign country would have been a source of great hilarity only a decade or so ago. Such can be the quirks of evolution.

August Aquila, a leading international consultant on accounting firm management (and my co-author of *Client at the Core*), says, "The traditional black box model of the all-knowing professional is now an anachronism. Where once clients didn't have access to the accounting process, accountants now function in collaboration with their clients. This has fostered, in many client matters, increasingly changing the client-professional relationship to one of consulting. This relationship continues to emerge as more aspects of the accounting process are commoditized, and are then outsourced. It's here, too, that technology serves as an important factor in accounting practice, as such practices as tax returns and bookkeeping are regularly sent to call centers in other countries, where they're processed by well-trained technicians."

This new kind of client is well known to the legal profession as well. Says

Pamela Waldow, "The language of many current RFPs now inclu
specific questions not just about a firm's legal expertise, but about how legal
services will be delivered, budgeted, monitored and managed. In-house
counsel are making clear what they want to pay and how they want services
delivered. Increasingly, they also have begun to insist that their outside law
firms provide additional no-cost perks."

New processes, such as defining, analyzing, and using data of all kinds
– knowledge management – are becoming an integral part of law and
accounting firm management, and are themselves evolving. Understanding
and using data and information – both internally for firm management and
externally as an aid to the crucial science and art of defining a market and
reaching it – is expanding. And now, we have dedicated knowledge management specialists, some of whom are lawyers or accountants, and some of
whom are data specialists, and many of whom are both professionals and
data specialists.

The firm that moves into the digital age – that uses technology with
increasing sophistication in all aspects of its business – is the new norm.
Increasingly, firm practices are shaped by technology. Processes are auto-
mated, the mobile office is becoming commonplace, concepts of productivity
are increasingly considered. Flex time and the internet allow people to work
at home, which helps keep talent and can improve productivity.

And marketing. And competition. Practice development? No longer
merely at the country club or golf course, but as a professional practice that's
integral to the professional firm's practice.

Bates v. State Bar of Arizona – and Professional Services Marketing 1.0

There seems to be a general impression that the changes in law and accounting practices that created the modern firm resulted from the blast of
technology that began to enter the professions in the early 1980s. Not so.
The current cycle of evolution resulting in the thread of change we now see
actually began in 1977, with the U.S. Supreme Court decision in *Bates v. State
Bar of Arizona*. The decision, which primarily addressed the subject of law
firm advertising, effectively upended generations of prohibitions against all
forms of promotion.

That landmark Supreme Court decision struck down the American Bar Association's Canons of Ethics, and by extension, the Code of Professional Conduct of The American Institute of CPAs, that for generations had inhibited frank marketing, or any form of commercialization, by professional firms. It profoundly altered the future of the accounting and legal professions, and started the evolutionary course that has led to the modern firm.

The ethical rules of the professions were ostensibly designed to preserve both the real and perceived probity and integrity of the professions. They obviated, as well, any deviations from the traditions of the practices, most of which fostered a virtual class war – a barrier between the all- knowing professional and the client. And while Bates specifically addressed lawyer advertising, ultimately the professionals realized that two things had happened – the decision applied to the accounting profession as well as to the legal profession, and the new concept of competition bred the first opportunities and efforts at marketing. Competition continues to be the driving force of evolution that defines the modern law and accounting firm, as it does for commercial enterprises.

Technology, of course, ultimately enhanced the evolutionary process, and continues to do so, but *competition*, not technology, drives the evolutionary process that portends continued change in the professions.

It took about five years before the true meaning of the *Bates* decision finally dawned on the professionals. The professionals gradually came to realize that the decision meant that, for the first time in the memory of most practitioners then alive, they could now openly solicit one another's clients – a practice that most professionals had never done before, nor had been allowed to do. It meant that the professionals had to face – and learn to deal with – not merely the polite and collegial competition of the past, but aggressive competition. Thus began a new course of practice, of professional firm management changes, and of a new process of professional services marketing. For many accountants and lawyers of that generation, it was painful. Moreover, it evoked that other fearful word, change .

In the attempt by professionals to find the path to successful marketing, for whom there was neither tradition nor experience in the marketing function, there was much groping. There were attempts to understand the concept of selling a service to people who might not immediately need it. Products are marketed to persuade consumers to buy now. Product marketing begins with the product, which is shaped to address not just the needs of the consumer, but the consumer's desires – whether known, perceived, or generated. Thus, in product marketing, defining, and even creating the product is as important as any other marketing techniques.

Differences Between Product and Professional Services Marketing

Lawyers and accountants have historically not been concerned with the market – they are concerned with being lawyers and accountants, and meeting their own personal needs for professionalism. They are concerned with merely getting clients. That was sufficient pre-Bates, but not now, because it's not a competitive approach in a seriously competitive environment. As the marketing consultant Janet Stanton has pointed out, and as the insightful work of consultants Donald Aronson and Larry Smith have shown, lawyers too often know too little about how clients choose lawyers from the vast roster of professionals – or even how clients perceive them. Surveys by the Bay Street Group have found the same for accounting firms.

The late corporate philosopher, Peter Drucker has often noted that the role of a corporation is to make a customer. Lawyers and accountants have the same ultimate responsibility – to generate a client – not merely to collect clients, but to build a viable practice. But the path to it is different from the role of marketing for products. Those differences significantly affect the nature and practices of law firm marketing. For example...

- **Product marketing sells products. Law and accounting firm marketing sell knowledge, capability and skills.** A product is static and defined in each iteration. A legal matter is dynamic, and frequently unique to each client.

- **Products have reliable consistency.** The next tube of your brand of toothpaste is exactly the same as the last tube you bought. The human element in a product is subsumed by the product. Lawyers' and accountants' performances vary case by case and by individual professionals, and are the essence of professional services.

- **Product manufacturers are able to generate customer need** where none existed before. Lawyers and accountants are constrained in their ability to create a need for their services where none had existed before (except to educate people about rights they didn't know they had, e.g. class action or personal injury, appealing a tax levy).

- **Product marketing has greater flexibility** to meet or shape the desires of the consumer. Professionals have little flexibility to work outside the structure of the law and legal process or the rules of accounting. A corporation can market test its product and the company can rapidly change it to adjust to customers' tastes. Professionals can't change the laws or accounting principles to suit the needs of their clients, despite the opportunity to be creative within the boundaries of the law or accounting principles.

- **There are flavors, emotional appeals, colors, and bells and whistles** that product marketers can use to distinguish a product from its competitors. Professionals are constrained by the law, by legal and accounting practice, and by ethical strictures. The adjectives of product marketing find little hospitality in professional services marketing.

- **There may be a thousand people,** and complex production processes, behind a product. The interface between these people and the consumer is the product itself. The interface between the professional and the *client* is the professional.

- **When a salesperson sells you a vacuum cleaner, the vacuum cleaner stays and the salesperson goes.** When a lawyer sells you his or her services, the professional stays.

- **Product marketing may specifically claim superiority** over competitive products, but while one professional may be smarter, more energetic, more reliable, and more imaginative than another, that professional can hardly promote that difference. You can't say, *"We write better briefs"* or *"We do better audits"* This is both an ethical and practical constraint, because you can't prove it.

- **The reputation of a law or accounting firm** can rise or fall on the performance of one lawyer or accountant and one client.

- **The product company is experienced,** with a long tradition in understanding its market and the concept of competing. It knows that it must actively define, pursue and nurture the consumer. Lawyers and accountants know that most clients have no choice but to use their services (nobody ever woke up and said, *"I think I'll sue somebody today"* or, *"What I really need today is a good audit"*). The word *competing* didn't seriously enter the lawyer's lexicon until 1977 (*Bates*) The product marketing tradition goes back centuries. There is virtually no active marketing or promotional tradition as we know it today for lawyers and accountants prior to 1977.

- **Product marketing can be measured by the number of products it sells.** But professional services marketing can ultimately have only three significant results – building name recognition and reputation, projecting capabilities that contribute to choosing one lawyer or accountant over another *when a lawyer or accountant is needed*, and gaining access to a prospect that affords the professional the opportunity to sell his or her services.

- **An ad campaign may drive a consumer to buy a product,** but it can't drive an individual or company to hire a lawyer or accounting firm. In professional services, the sale must be done by the professional, even when a non-professional supplies the access to the prospect.

- **The product company understands that no matter what product** it makes, it is really a marketing company that manufactures products to fill the channel opened by marketing activities. Lawyers and accountants too often see themselves, not their consumers (clients), at the center of their universe. Too bad. When professionals begin to understand that basic marketing concept, the earth will shake, walls will crumble, and the practice of law and accounting will change. But it will still be ethical and the public will be better served.

- **Ultimately, a product is an abstraction – a symbol. It can be changed or replaced at the manufacturer's whim, in response to a changing customer's whim.** Last year's Kewpie doll is replaceable by next year's Barbie Doll – all in response to the market's whim. The law is the law and accounting principles are immutable. There may be flexibility in application, or sometimes in imaginative approaches, but not at the whim or the client.

- **If you sell a product, you're selling against competition.** If you sell a process (such as a legal or accounting solution), you're selling against (or to) the customer's needs.

What Does This Tell Us?

Experience in functioning in this realm of differences tells us that law and accounting firm marketing can work when it's designed to...

- **Enhance name recognition and reputation** as a context for other marketing activities, and specifically, selling. In all areas of marketing, these two factors are particularly meaningful

- **Project skills and expertise** as the best way to distinguish one firm from another

- **Enhance access to prospective clients,** and ultimately, to sell

- **Shape a practice to conform to your firm's business plan**

- **Address constantly changing marketing needs,** dictated by new laws, new business structures, or new technology

- **Effectively sell** skills and capabilities to the prospects

To accomplish these objectives, then, the tools of marketing – seminars, speeches, public relations, advertising, articles, the social media, selling skills etc. – must be tailored within the framework of projecting expertise. This also means that the adjectives and comparisons and superlatives so common in product marketing have no place in professional services marketing. The boast, even when there seems to be a foundation for it, rarely works.

A typical example of this process at work is in a direct mail letter or other direct response or targeted marketing campaigns. While most products may be sold directly in response to a direct response campaign, the well-crafted direct response campaign for lawyers has the sole objective of generating the opportunity for the professional to make a personal presentation. The sale is made in person, usually by the lawyer or accountant who will serve the client.

Long ago, for a large international accounting firm, I developed a four paragraph system that produced a return of 50% – 50% of the recipients of the campaign agreed to meet with us. In paragraph one, we stated the problem in the most dire way we could. Paragraph two said, *"we can help."* Paragraph three said *"this is who we are."* Paragraph four said *"we'll call you on Monday to set up an appointment."* And 50% of the letters' recipients agreed to meet. Yes, 50%.

Professional services marketing, then, is designed to move prospective clients to understand that when the need for legal or accounting services does arise, they should choose the *marketer's firm* rather than another. Retaining a lawyer or an accountant is rarely a discretionary purchase. Buying a product, in many cases, is. Product marketing can persuade people to try a new product, or that your product is better than the other person's. But you're not likely to persuade someone to get an audit that isn't externally demanded, or through marketing, to persuade a happily married person to get a divorce. There are claims and promises you can't credibly make in professional services marketing. This new competitive paradigm called for a new and unfamiliar form of form of marketing, and a new kind of marketer. In every industry save one, the marketing department joins the other disciplines to help shape the product – not just its presentation, but the product itself. It's the marketing department that is responsible for knowing the pulse of the market, and to shape products or services the market needs or will respond to. This is a crucial part of marketing products and non-profit services. The exception is professional services.

In those early days, the firms reluctantly hired people they thought were professional marketers. For example, one then-Big Eight accounting firm hired an advertising firm executive who, it turned out, had been in ad agency production, and knew nothing about marketing. Another firm hired a public relations company that saw all marketing as public relations. Public relations or advertising people were hired who didn't have the least idea of how law and accounting firms worked. How could the professionals know otherwise? Professional marketing and its process were new to the lawyers and accountants, and they had never hired marketers before

At first, the newly minted marketers tried to use the same techniques used to market products. Some professionals were even persuaded that people who know how to market products would know how to market professional services. They didn't.

Product marketers had been marketing for generations, but lawyers and accountants, without a sound marketing tradition, had to learn it from scratch. There were many obstacles. There was as well the intense need to make clear the role of marketing and the nature of marketers. To most professionals, after decades in which marketing was not only prohibited, but was considered unprofessional and even unsavory, the marketers and their practices were accepted only reluctantly, and as completely ancillary to law or accounting firm practices. The nature, training and mindset of the marketer seemed to be inimical to that of lawyers and accountants.

The professionals felt that marketing was undignified, and that those who did it were themselves less than dignified. They saw marketing as hucksterism, and certainly not in the professional services tradition. This, despite the fact that the professions are the only commercial enterprise that demand the participation of the practitioners to run a marketing effort. Without the input of the lawyers and accountants, there's no grist for the marketing mill.

But the worst part was the disconnect between the professionals and the marketers. This disconnect was – and to a lesser extent, still is – a significant factor in slowing the development of professional services marketing techniques. The professionals, whose only knowledge of marketing was the casually observed and often misconstrued product marketing structure, in which marketing was distinctly separate from the manufacturing process, assumed that they had nothing to do with marketing or marketers. They assumed that marketing was done by outsiders who were not part of the legal or accounting professions, and they were frequently dismissive of both the marketers and the process. This recalcitrant attitude persisted throughout the next three decades – *Marketing 2.0*. In many ways, this attitude informed the nature of the relationship of both the marketing and the professional practice.

Bates started the evolution from the traditions of the past to a new paradigm in professional services. This period of turmoil, from which came the beginnings of organized professional services marketing, and the foundation for the modern firm, was *Professional Services Marketing 1.0*.

But ultimately, the lawyers and accountants gradually came to understand that marketing was inevitable, if only because their competitors were doing it. Because of this new competition, the lawyers and accountants simply lost the option. They had to market. It was a time of learning, of accommodating, and even of acquiescing.

Subsequently, the firms and the marketers came to understand which marketing techniques worked for professional services, and which didn't. Gradually, the professionals began to understand what marketing was, and how it worked to help them compete. With experience, and a refinement of techniques, this became *Professional Services Marketing 2.0*.

Professional Services Marketing 2.0

In the years following *Bates*, both law and accounting firms began a long and difficult process of learning how to market.

Lawyers and accountants were still so steeped in the no-commercialization ethic that they tried to resist any form of marketing. They couldn't, because other firms had started doing it, and were winning clients.

It was in this period that the traditional concepts of anti-marketing began to erode, and the professions began to change. Subtly, and barely perceptively, they began to understand that the purpose of a business enterprise, including a professional firm, is to create a customer – a client. These definitions flaunt generations of traditional anti-promotional attitudes. They said, essentially, that law and accounting firms are merely a vehicle to bring law and accounting to a public that needs these services. Like any business enterprise, marketing opens the channels to its customers. The professional fills these channels with professional services as needed.

It's taken almost four decades, since *Bates*, for the processes of professional services marketing to mature, and to become a legitimate and integral part of professional services practice.

It was the evolution of this concept that precipitated change to meet the needs of reaching the prospective client.

Learning to Market

In this second phase of marketing – *Professional Services Marketing 2.0* – we learned to better understand the profound distinctness and uniqueness of marketing a professional service. We learned to adapt the traditional tools of product marketing to the unique uses of those tools, mechanics, and strategies in professional services marketing. We learned, slowly, a new body of marketing techniques and new ways to use traditional marketing practices.

As the marketing techniques were refined, and the number of law and accounting firm marketers increased, the marketing techniques became a catalogue of practices that constituted a litany – a compendium of universal professional services marketing practices. With no formal training structures in professional services marketing, and with universities teaching only product marketing, marketers had to learn from one another. (*The Marcus Letter*, both in hard copy [pre-internet] and online, was among the first publications to chronicle these new techniques, and in some cases, to adapt or invent them.) With few professional services academic courses, but input from often clueless professionals, marketers had to learn from one another, which, with few exceptions, did little to refine or develop new techniques. These marketing mechanics became institutionalized, with some refinement, embellishment, and experience, but unfortunately, little subsequent innovation.

The standard practices were then imposed on the law and accounting firms, virtually by rote. There were, of course, exceptions, and brilliant and original executions of standard and universal practices, but they were indeed exceptions. The problem was that with thousands of marketers all doing the same things, competing was often diluted.

In most law and accounting firm marketing, we take what's given to us from the practice, and impose marketing techniques on the firm and its services. Traditionally there is little or no input by marketers to help shape the service being promoted. This results in marketing by rote, where ultimate marketing performance is driven by factors not entirely within the control of the marketers. I've long called this the Melancholy Baby Syndrome – the piano player who'll play Melancholy Baby no matter what you really want to hear. Too many law and accounting firm marketers barely understand the nature of the practice, and the lawyers and accountants who practice it. Granted, the law itself is at the base of law firm practice, as are the strictures of accounting – but the ways in which that service can be described and delivered function with some latitude. With the same limited tools available to all firms, with the same inhibitions imposed on all marketers, the tools to compete are as limited as if all artists had to paint only in black and white.

In 1980, in what was probably the first post-Bates article on Marketing 2.0, I wrote on marketing an accounting firm for the Virginia Society of Accountants (see Chapter 9). Revisiting that article today I'm stunned to see that to a large degree virtually every word is not only still relevant today, but that little has been added to the basics outlined in the article. This, despite the rapid and vast proliferation of professional services marketers, and the extensive introduction and use of new technology. Yes, there have been refinements and embellishments, and even some ingenious and imaginative use of marketing techniques. But the techniques – and most significantly, the relationship between most lawyers and accountants and most marketers who serve them, have been virtually the same as it had been since the 1980s.

The problem is that in that interim period from about 1980 to now, the practices of law and accounting – techniques, governance, client relation-ships – have changed substantially, as have the economy and the markets for these services, but the techniques of marketing professional services have remained static. The article I wrote in 1980 is still current.

But now, the lawyers and accountants have been and are becoming more sophisticated. The nature of the market for their services is changing, as is the nature of professional services practices. Marketing 2.0 has been losing its grip, and return on marketing investment has been too difficult to discern by skeptical lawyers and accountants. And tenure for marketers continues to be short, with frequent turnover. Reading the resumes of any ten marketers today is to see a catalogue of American law and accounting firms – a game of musical chairs. But still, there have been exceptions – and they sowed the seeds of the next generation of marketing to serve the changing needs of the marketplace – Marketing 3.0.

Professional Services Marketing 3.0

Now, we begin to enter a new phase of marketing, in which marketing is not only integrated into the practice, but actually helps shape the nature of the practice itself. This is marketing 3.0. It is characterized by marketers – professional marketers, lawyers, accountants, firm managers – who fully understand the nature of legal or accounting practice, as well as the techniques and skills of marketing professional services. These marketers often go well beyond the practices of Marketing 2.0.

There is a new generation of lawyers and accountants who, unlike their predecessors during marketing 2.0, fully understand that marketing is as much part of the practice as billing and other financial controls. Even the process of the growing field of knowledge management, long considered primarily technical for acquiring and managing internal data as a management function, is now beginning to include marketing data as integral to managing a firm. And why not? No professional firm exists without its clients.

Where once project management was taken for granted, there is now a more sophisticated approach to it, as part of a growing firm management professionalism needed to improve productivity.

The older generation felt that *Bates*, and the competition it introduced, was the death knell of the professions. Quite the opposite, it turned out, has proven to be true. Competition has sharpened the practice, and helped introduce new services that better serve both the firms and the clients. The changes, when compared to the firms of the pre-*Bates* era, are phenomenal. It has led to more streamlined firm management and service structures, benefiting both the firm and its clients.

It's a new partnership between the professionals, who are imbued with a true understanding of the meaning of marketing to a contemporary practice and their inevitable role in it, and marketers who fully understand the markets and services, and the personalities of lawyers and accountants.

If the marketers of Marketing 2.0 better understood the craft and tools of marketing professional services, the marketers of 3.0 better understand the practice of law or accounting, including each profession's disciplines, fundamental characteristics and tasks in the actual practice of law or accounting, as well as the distinctive personality traits of lawyers and accountants. At the same time, the professionals of 2.0 now better understand the principles and practices of marketing – Professional Services Marketing 3.0.

Ultimately, Marketing 3.0 is impelled by several factors...

- Today's lawyers and accountants understand that, unlike most other occupations, they must be active participants in the process, at least as suppliers of grist for the marketing mills, and certainly as part of the ultimate selling process. What's more significant is that they begin to see the professionalism in marketing, and particularly the selling aspect of it. Says Halloran & Sage's Chief Operating Officer, David Urbanik, "Successful business development in a law firm also requires a third dimension – business risk and financial analyses." This, he says, is particularly significant in such areas as fee negotiation, and in helping to design business solutions.

- With the new configurations of law firms evolving, both lawyers and accountants and the marketers who serve them have greater reason to work more closely. Says David Urbanik, "Case management systems and well defined communication protocols that insure consistency of approach and fee arrangements that give a high degree of certainty as to the costs of services rendered can often be the deciding factor in retaining legal services. Thus, the truth of the old adage, 'Clients do not hire law firms, they hire lawyers' may be fading. In more and more markets, they actually do hire law firms. The consistency of approach and certainty of cost that clients are seeking may not be that far from the consistency expected by the purchaser of the tube of toothpaste. – something to think about." True, but on the other hand, most people still hire skills, whether they perceive them in individual lawyers or in entire firms.

- Today's marketers and professionals are both beginning to have a better understanding of the markets themselves, and the industries in which clients function. They know the difference between understanding the elements of a market versus simply segmenting mailing lists. They are more conversant with the techniques of fathoming market needs, and designing not only marketing programs, but firm structures to better meet those needs. They better understand how to shape services to meet client demands and needs.

- Because of their ability to understand consumers, product marketers not only feed market information back to their companies, they also are significant contributors to the design and development of new products. With a few exceptions, this has rarely been the practice under 2.0. Under 3.0, more and more marketers will participate in designing new services for clients, as well as the programs to market those services. In fact, marketers are increasingly responsible for understanding the market and feeding market information back to the firm.

- This new generation of lawyers and accountants better understands their clients' businesses and industries. This results in improved client service and relationships, and therefore better practice of law and accounting.

- An increased focus on selling – both by the professionals and the marketers, has produced a new generation of specialists. While selling has always been part of the marketing process, competition has bred a new focus on its importance and skills, to the point that the specialists are trained practitioners of what is now called, appropriately, Practice Development. The thoughtful marketing consultant, Suzanne Lowe, made extensive inroads into the art and craft of the process in her recent book, *The Integration Imperative: Erasing Marketing Business Development Silos- Once and for All - in Professional Service Firms.*

- In many respects, the practices of law and accounting intertwine. For example, estate planning draws upon both law and accounting practices. While we seem to be light years away from the two professions physically merging under one banner, they often serve overlapping constituencies. The marketer of 3.0 will have a profound understanding of both practices.

Marketing 2.0 evolved as marketing for lawyers and accountants matured, and the marketing practices we use today became standard, and somewhat sophisticated – if not universally so. Except now, Marketing 3.0 is emerging. It is evolving – and gives us a better clue to the future of the profession than all the prognostication of the self-proclaimed seers. If the professionals of Marketing 2.0 misconceived marketing and marketers, the professionals of Marketing 3.0 now begin to see themselves as partners with marketers – active, contributing partners. What had been an us-them relationship is becoming a professional/marketer partnership.

Typical proponents of this new form of marketing are lawyers and accountants who have learned to think and act like marketers, lawyers and accountants who have developed new kinds of law and accounting firms, and new kinds of governance structures. It's a system that in at least one aspect draws upon a product marketing practice – in that the marketers participate in designing aspects of legal and accounting practice. It's a system in which lawyers relate to clients in more constructive ways, and in dialogues rather than monologues. In law and accounting firms in which the barriers between partners and associates who are skilled and talented have eroded, and client service teams that not only serve clients better, but function as marketing instruments, by virtue of developing better ways of demonstrating the possibilities of extended service.

Some Examples

David Urbanik is one such individual functioning under Marketing 3.0. Neither a lawyer nor a trained professional marketer, no lawyer or marketer better understands both the legal profession and its practices, as well as the art of practice development. Urbanik pointed out that…"Product companies do market research and alter their products to better fit what their customers need or desire. Traditionally, professional service firms look at markets and attempt to deliver services they have to the opportunities they see." Maybe the shifting paradigm, he says, is the need for professionals to listen more carefully to clients and change what they do and how they do it (shape a product/service)) in response to what they hear.

And, notes Urbanik, "You can't shape something if you don't understand it and can't communicate clearly with those who must be at the core of building it... meeting the explicit or implicit client need which very well may require something different from the traditional law firm model."

Working with Urbanik, we added a new marketing component to the firm's practice groups. This not only enhanced each group's marketing efforts, but helped build a firm marketing culture. We then focused marketing efforts on those prospects and markets with the greatest potential for growth and profitability, without totally ignoring those at the other end of the spectrum. The emphasis is on focused. It worked.

In the brochure and web site we did, we broke our services into groups that addressed the specific need of clients – what they needed – not merely what we had to sell off the shelf. Thus, we spoke of meeting the needs of clients in areas of Value Creation, Operational Support, Transactional Support, Risk Management, Preventative Law, Asset Recovery, Litigation Services, and Wealth Preservation and Distribution. In other words, we tailored our product – these categories – in terms of the client's needs and opportunities, not just laundry lists of our services.

In this context, the need to bring a firm's capabilities to the market is resulting in new kinds of firms, structured to address and serve the markets for its services. These new firms focus on client service, and firm productivity, without in any way diminishing professional integrity

Examples

Outstanding examples of the new kind of law and accounting firms arising in this context are Shepherd Law Group, Valorem Law Group, Kellogg & Andelson, Exemplar Law Partners, Seiler LLP, and Axiom Legal. They have in common a drive to remake the law and accounting firm business models to better and more economically serve clients. Their focus is on putting the client, rather than the practice and the firm, at the core of their business model.

Ronald Baker, Founder of the Consulting firm and think tank VeraSage, was a pioneer and early advocate of value pricing (which is most often at the core of the contemporary firm), including considerable original thinking on the definition of the concept of value to a client, for both law and accounting firms. A former accountant – he started a career as a junior accountant in the former Big Eight accounting firm, Peat, Marwick Mitchell (as did I, a decade or more earlier, and in a different capacity) , and has been a driving force in persuading firms to consider value pricing. Where it's used most successfully, it's based on his models, which are then further adapted firm by firm.

The contemporary law firm is epitomized in the Boston-based Shepherd Law Group, both in concept and in practice. Specializing in employment law and litigation, it was started some 13 years ago by Jay Shepherd. About eight years ago, functioning on value-based principles delineated by Ron Baker, Shepherd abandoned the hourly billing format to develop a workable system of ascertaining the value of his service to his client and billing accordingly.

Value pricing, says Shepherd, is more than just a replacement of the anachronistic hourly billing system – it's a manifestation of understanding the meaning of value – but value to the client, before the considerations of the firm. The result is not only satisfied clients, but increased profit for the firm. At the same time, says Shepherd, value pricing impels the firm to avoid unnecessary processes – to be more efficient.

The Shepherd Law Group is a small firm, but they are leading specialists in employment law and litigation. While it's been said that a litigation practice is difficult to price by value rather than by billable hours, Shepherd has clearly demonstrated how it can be done, particularly where a firm's expertise supplies the knowledge and experience. He is the firm's owner, with no other partners, and functions with a small staff of specialists. This form of operating, he says, is a paradigm that breaks a mold, and that functions particularly well.

Interestingly, Shepherd disdains the term "alternate billing", particularly because it assumes that the other alternative is the billable hour The problem with the billable hour, he and others have pointed out, is that if there's any value in hourly billing, it's to the firm, not the client. To perform a service to clients with no value to clients is to be anti-competitive – particularly with today's sophisticated clients.

Shepherd's use of value pricing is so effective that he has established a subsidiary operation, called PreFix, to both teach other firms how to do it and to consult to, and advise, law and accounting firms on specific pricing problems. His 14 points of how to determine a value price are widely known, and increasingly used by other firms, both in the United States and abroad.

Those points are…

1. I analyze the client
2. I assess the importance of the situation
3. I assess the urgency of the situation
4. I pay attention to what my competitors charge
5. I consider the relative values of each possible outcome
6. I figure out how hard it would be for the client to get better service elsewhere
7. I determine how important my firm's expertise is to the likelihood of a successful outcome (in other words, is this going to be easier because of our particular skills, or could any monkey on the internet find the answers
8. I consider what we charged other clients in the past for similar work
9. I consider whether those charges were heavy or light in retrospect
10. I consider the likelihood of getting more work from this client
11. I assess how much work we've done for this client already
12. I wonder how important getting this particular job is to our firm (if it isn't, I might raise the price)
13. I decide whether to do a single price for the whole gig, or how to break up the job into mini-gigs with separate prices
14. Then I say, "This is our price."

Valorem was founded in 2008 by the noted attorney Patrick Lamb, and several like-minded attorneys (now five) – all of whom saw the traditional law firm model as less than relevant to the changing needs of the contemporary clientele. Their objective in starting the firm was to find ways to improve client service at reasonable fees. They too function with value billing. The five lawyers are all partners, all with equal compensation. Lamb is widely known for his work as a practicing attorney and, particularly, for client service. There is a freedom from the traditional top-down pyramid law firm to a firm more concerned with client service than the formalities of the traditional firm. This approach is enhanced by the elimination of the billable hour, and a focus on value – both in resolving client needs and problems, and in billing.

One of the foremost thinkers and practitioners in the legal profession, Patrick Lamb has been a pioneer in alternative, value-based fees. As a founder of Valorem Law Group, he is also a pioneer in new forms of management and governance for the contemporary firm. His book, published by Managing Partner Magazine, is *Alternative Fee Arrangements: Value Fees and the Changing Legal Market*, (Ark, $450.00). It demonstrates the new perspective of lawyers who think beyond the traditional practice formats, and is one of the most comprehensive discussions of the subject. It's based upon Lamb's extensive experience in the process. More than merely a primer, it explores concepts of value, and different pricing models, and their effect on a practice, and particularly on client service. Its concepts are the foundation on which Valorem is built, and is having a profound impact on the emergence of value billing as a replacement for the billable hour.

In an extensive article in his outstanding blog, Adam Smith, Esq., (Bruce MacEwen), reports that Exemplar Law Partners was started in 2006 by Christopher Marston, who was fresh out of law school. Dissatisfied with what he saw as an outdated law firm model, including the cumbersome billable hour and top-down management structure, he felt that no one, least of all the clients, benefited from the traditional standards. His firm hires lawyers with business degrees or extensive industry experience and a team orientation. It offers a clients service guarantee. And significantly, it has been an enthusiastic marketer since its inception. Among the innovative practices (at least for law firms) he has adopted are…

- Billing only on the basis of fixed prices – fees are determined for each project by a pricing committee, which addresses each engagement individually
- Offering clients a satisfaction guarantee
- Hiring only lawyers with business degrees or with extensive industry

experience
- Hiring ultra-selectively. Among the criteria new hires must have are social graces, an interest in and confidence to develop new business, a team orientation, and the willingness to risk their own compensation from day one by accepting no guarantee of starting salary in exchange for profit-sharing participation.

- Making an "over-investment" in an experienced management team from non-lawyer backgrounds – the COO has many years of experience in banking, while the CMO has many years of experience in various industries, most recently in direct sales. "I sought out varied backgrounds for a new, fresh approach," Marston says. Instituting a "No Grinch" teamwork approach.

Since its inception, Exemplar has grown to six offices, serving the mid-market legal profession. Moreover, it has expanded into investment banking, raising capital for clients and other businesses, taking the concept of the business-oriented law firm into new dimensions.

Of all the emerging changes in the professional world, perhaps none is as innovative as is the accounting firm Kellogg & Andelson, which substantially breaks the traditional mold of the accounting profession.

Founded in the late 1930s as a traditional accounting firm, it's now run by Christian Payne, a former investment banker. Payne is not a CPA, but is now able to function as the head of an accounting firm under recent rules that allow partners who are not CPAs to be partners if they don't own a majority of the firm.

Two things distinguish the contemporary K&A – they do no auditing, but function with captive operations in India, having a web-based firm of CPAs, under the banner of CPAFlex, and with acquired affiliates. K&A itself just does taxes and write-ups, neither of which have to be done by CPAs, and consulting by a highly experienced group of accountants and business specialists. They outsource their work to their captive Indian subsidiary, while retaining senior technical capability.

They partner as well with independent CPA firms, whose work is carefully managed by the parent company, but still allow the associated firms to function professionally. In addition to supervision that controls quality, they supply both intellectual and marketing services, staffing, technology, and training. Their Flexible Retirement Program, for example, allows accounting firm owners approaching retirement to continue running their practices, earning income based on billable hours while concurrently getting paid out of their practice.

Based in Southern California, they continue to acquire CPA firms in their CPAFlex subsidiary. Looking to the future, Payne, who has built the firm in large measure through carefully managed acquisitions, anticipates the possibility of ultimately taking the firm public, which is already being seriously discussed in Great Britain. While external sources of equity capital may be a long time coming for the professions, it may prove necessary when rapid growth – particularly through mergers and acquisition – require more capital than can be supplied by partners or banks and other lenders.

Axiom Legal was started in 2000 as a virtual law firm by Mark Harris, a then-29 year old associate in a large New York law firm. It's one that functions without the trappings of the traditional law firm structure or large offices. Relying on a large network of attorneys recruited from major law firms, they offer experience and service without the high fees of firms with real estate to house high priced partners. Clients are often served with teams of lawyers with different but relevant specialties. It's focus is on value for the clients, rather than the traditional trappings of the old model law firm. The firm has grown to nine offices, including London and Hong Kong. This new business model, designed to meet the changing needs of clients, has grown rapidly, and portends the likelihood of the law firm business model of the future.

Gale Crosley, a thoughtful and pioneering consultant, reports in the accounting publication, *Accounting Today*, that one of the leading and innovative accounting firms she has encountered is a 53-year old firm that is on the leading edge of the profession – Redwood City, California-based Seiler LLP.

Traditionally specializing in real estate-oriented, multi-generational family enterprises, when it was struck by the real estate bubble in the late 1980s, managing partner Jim DeMartini responded by going after Silicon Valley high-tech companies, and restructuring the firm to streamline its competitive advantage. DiMartini, Crosley reports, is convinced that business development is a skill that can be learned, and demonstrated it by growing what is now a 15-partner $33 million firm. Its growth is entirely internal, rather than by acquisition.

Clients are served by carefully structured teams with technical expertise that includes tax and estate planning. Clients prefer teams with a blend of appropriate knowledge and skills to serve them, rather than by a single individual, according to DiMartini. Says Crosley, "Members are assessed on their long-term value to the organization, and not for their most recent acquisition of a promising client. Equity ownership is based on career performance as well."

The rapidly growing firm has about 140 individuals in two locations – Redwood City and San Francisco. The firm functions with high levels of client satisfaction and very low rates of client and employee turnover. Building from within, says Crosley, helps ensure that the firm's younger members will have a place to thrive.

Cravens & Cravens, a former client of mine, is a two-person father and son accounting firm in a small town in Southern Illinois, with growth ambitions, and a keen understanding of the role of marketing in its practice. Their one advantage was an exceptional knowledge of small and medium size business. We marketed the firm by focusing on that capability and by featuring the rolling forecast and the firm's business acumen, rather than on the traditional small accounting firm services. It's been a very successful concept and campaign, made possible by the two partners' willingness to reach beyond traditional accounting practice techniques.

That the contemporary firms, such as those described here, tend to use value pricing is no surprise. In today's competitive environment, anything but a firm structured to give value to its clients, as does value pricing, is not likely to long sustain against its competitors. The question is which came first – the contemporary firm or value pricing?

Actually, it's a moot point. Breaking from the traditional billable hour requires a mindset that tends to function with not only the client at the core of the practice, but with an eye to improved productivity. And while exploring a concept like measuring the value of a service to clients is a sharp break from the past (not only for the firm, but for clients as well, although experience indicates that once they understand the process, clients readily accept it), it's not all that difficult for a firm to adopt. In both legal and accounting practices, changing a business model is often a form of defensive practice, particularly when competitors are doing it successfully. This is the way of the evolution of ideas.

At a recent VeraSage conference, Ron Baker addressed the question of why no top 100 accounting or law firm has switched to value billing. He notes that major firms that are national and international advertisers use time sheets in compensating their ad agencies.

But the answer, he points out, is not difficult to discern. "There are decades of culture," he says, "around the culture of timesheets." They are literally at the center of all financial reporting in the firm, and there is too much investment in timesheets and related financial systems for senior management to move in different directions. "It's human nature to remain on the shores of the familiar," he says. As for the future of value billing, he is optimistic, as am I.

Much of my thinking about finding ways to use successful product marketing techniques and business practices came from Peter Drucker, who said, "If you think of yourself as a marketing company that fills the channels of marketing you open with the products you make, you have vast expansion opportunities." Thus, many years ago, when I was with a major public relations firm (Ruder & Finn), and Bissell Carpet Sweeper was my client. We realized that they were missing an opportunity to thrive in a new marketing-oriented environment. "Right now," we agreed, "you are just a manufacturing company. You make carpet sweepers. You call in your sales force and say, 'Yesterday we made X number of carpet sweepers. Today you have to sell X number of carpet sweepers.'"

I said. "You have a great sales force. Ask them to come back with ideas of what their customers want and would buy if you could manufacture them." Company president Mel Bissell agreed, and thus was born the Bissell ShampooMaster, followed by several other products. He hired a detergent chemist from Dow, and his shop foreman designed the machine. And thus began a whole line of home cleaning products. Bissell, once just a manufacturer, became a marketing company.

These are examples of a new generation and a new approach to marketing professional services that successfully adapted the practice of law and accounting to specifically meet the needs of clients.

While all selling must ultimately be done by the lawyer or accountant, the practice of practice development, incorporating as it may the traditional tools of marketing, will be done either by a lawyer or accountant, or a business-oriented person who is totally immersed in the practice, and has the skills and knowledge to reshape aspects of the practice – how it is presented and how it delivers its services – to better meet the needs of the contemporary client.

I know that an increasing number of successful law and accounting firms today are doing pretty much what I've described here. Some of the best marketers are lawyers or accountants. Some of the worst are, too. But the marketing profession is defined by its best – not its worst.

Under Marketing 3.0, practice development executives will have business, not just marketing, backgrounds. Marketing mechanics will be done by lower level practitioners, while the strategies will be formulated by the Marketing 3.0 specialists – the professional/marketers partners.

What has changed here is a new kind of professional services marketing, in response to new market needs, and the need to compete under these new circumstances. What is changing as well is a new kind of partnership between the professionals and those who market their services.

That's Marketing 3.0.

{Chapter 2}

Change Is A Result-Evolution Is The Process

The Anatomy Of Getting To Professional Services Marketing 3.0 – And Beyond

It's not difficult to understand, in this economic environment, why the word change looms so large in professional services dialogue. The nature of the professions, rooted as they are in history and tradition, can be fairly rigid, and resistant to innovation. But the times seem to have accelerated the need for new ideas and structures to cope with new economic and social problems and opportunities.

The accounting profession, even as we know it today, is practically pre-historic, and is now so bound by traditions, rules, regulations, and laws, that any suggestion of serious structural change is seen as a virtual assault on the professions. The codification of laws and the legal profession go back about as far, and are just as resistant to innovation. In both cases, the rigidity in the professions is designed to maintain integrity and probity, as well as efficiency in firm governance. If the nature of products allows for constant and rapid change to match changing tastes and fashions, the nature of professional services requires a measure of uniformity and predictability. But now, there are cracks appearing in the wall. The potential for conflict between the ethical rules and their protection of integrity, and the need for successful competitive marketing, can be intense.

Still, some things in the professions are different now than they were about a decade ago. We now have, for example, an increasing number of firms replacing hourly billing with value billing. We now have social media and we have technology. Law firm governance is beginning to resemble corporate structure, and indeed, there is talk of law firms going public (which I predicted about two decades ago when it became clear that the growth of the professions would require infusion of more capital than could be supplied by the partnership. This is the kind of situation that begins an evolutionary process.) Where once associates who seemed not to be partner material were let go, now they are being kept for their specific talents and experience – the so-called two-tier firm.

The accounting profession, recognizing the growth of globalization, is now seriously considering international accounting standards. (I helped run a vast international conference in England on the subject some two decades ago, and wrote a book on it with Columbia University's John Burton. And they're just beginning to act on it?) The changes in professional firm practices seem to be coming fast, and continue to do so, giving rise to the Professional Services Marketing 3.0 described in the last chapter.

And as we noted in Chapter 1, the clientele for both professions has changed substantially.

These things didn't happen by accident, nor by just an inspiration by a few bright lawyers or accountants. They are the result of an evolutionary process – which is *change*.

What, Exactly, Is Change

In the context of professional services practice and marketing, change is alteration of a process, practice, or condition that varies from the past.

First, for all the talk about change, and all the writing and talking and handwringing about change, it becomes clear that too many professionals see change as an event, finite, an end in itself. In fact, change is not an *event* that's arbitrarily made to happen, but a *process* – the result of which is that something changes. Most often, and with rare exceptions, that process leads to an evolution, and sometimes, even revolution (such as professional firm advertising, long forbidden – now common).

Second, change is inevitable. It's going to happen, whether we like it or not. Why? Because the events that contribute to change are too many to control or resist. They come from too many sources, motivated by too many external and unpredictable factors. We can learn to accommodate to the courses of action that portend change, but we cannot control it. In fact, as state bar and accounting associations are discovering, some change can't even be impeded by fiat or legislation. They keep trying, though.

Third, change, in the professions and in marketing professional services, isn't often deliberately made – it evolves slowly in response to external stimuli. Except for a few visionaries, like Ron Baker of the VeraSage Institute and an early proponent of value billing, Shepherd Law Group's Jay Shepherd, Exemplar Law Partner's Christopher Marston, K&A's Christian Payne, Axiom Legal's Mark Harris, and Valorem's Patrick Lamb, who anticipated the future in areas such as billing structures and firm governance, for most professionals change most often comes in response to changing needs of the marketplace, which demand new practices and new structures to serve those needs. Electronic media, for example, wasn't invented to change the practice of law or accounting – but it served to instigate change in those professions. And not overnight, either. It certainly was a response to the need to compete in an increasingly competitive market. (But that competitive market was virtually created in 1977, with *Bates*. It's taken all this time for responses in both the professional chambers and in marketing to evolve.) Social media began as just that – social. But it evolved into a competitive tool by virtue of its easy ability to communicate to large numbers of people, as well as to individuals, which makes it a natural instrument of change. It was useful because it circumvented the rigors of external control of the message, which happens in the print media, and has a broader and more immediate reach than does the traditional media. Opportunity, then, precipitates change. Social media, new kid on the block as it was, significantly changed marketing from the seller shouting down to the prospective consumer, to a two-way conversation between the seller and the consumer. The impact of that change is still evolving.

Another example of change is value pricing, which has been touted for decades, and is only now emerging as a viable practice. Firm governance, and the traditional top-down firm management that's long been the tradition in professional firms, is slowly, slowly emerging in new forms that better serve a practice's ability to help clients. The concept of *value* now becomes a major issue, which undoubtedly will result in further change, as firms struggle to define it. And if you can't define it, how do you bill for it? Client service teams are emerging to replace the eat-what-you-kill culture, in which each individual in a firm is his or her own entrepreneur. On the horizon today is the corporately owned or public professional firm.

I point this out, not to carp, but to wonder, and to consider, how this process can be dealt with competitively, and whether there is an initiative that can be taken to stay ahead of the curve.

There are two main areas in which change is imminent in the professions – firm structures and practices that allow a firm to better serve the needs of its clients, and marketing that's consistent with the clients' changing economic environment. Both are necessary for competitive reasons, both are imminent in order to keep a firm relevant to the dynamic changes in the world of both commerce and society. (There are, at the same time, many changes that occur daily as a result of new laws and regulations, but these are promulgated in response to external factors that precipitated the new laws, such as *Sarbanes-Oxley*.)

Evolution

We live in a dynamic world, in which constant motion of events and social and economic structures continually alter the state of many activities and circumstances. For example, the advent of the personal computer in 1981 changed the way trade and commerce were done. This altered the nature of financial structures, industrial practices and communications. But it also gave rise to new laws and new needs in accounting and finance. It created a new business environment that affected all participants in the cycles. It's an ongoing cycle that generates new problems and needs in many disciplines, including law and accounting. New financial instruments, new laws and regulations, new technology that accelerates the pace of doing business, growing internationalism, the expanding body of knowledge in so many areas and the rapidity with which it can be organized and retrieved, new demands from client – all substantially change the demands upon lawyers and accountants, and therefore, the structures and practices that professionals must adopt to stay abreast of their own clients.

I think that in order to understand change, you have to start by recognizing that change is an evolutionary process, the result of which is that some thing or things are different than they had hitherto been.

It's important to recognize as well the dynamic of today's society, in which events are impacted – sometimes randomly – by other events that are themselves impacted by unforeseeable events, and so on – all of which makes it impossible to accurately and consistently forecast. Perhaps a simpler way to see this is what I call the address in space.

My Address in Space

If you ask me where I live, I tell you that I live on the corner of X and Y Streets. It was there yesterday, it's there today, and will be there tomorrow. But I live on a planet in space that's constantly in motion, as are the other planets in our orbit. My address in space, then, is always in relation to the other planets in orbit, and therefore, constantly changing.

This dynamic between planets in motion exists between ideas and events as well, and is a major factor in the evolutionary process of change. This is how the evolutionary process works to create change...

...Competition leads to...

...Responsiveness to the marketplace, which leads to...

...Professional marketers, who are affected by...

...Changing needs of clients (usually in their response to changing economic and social conditions, such as new laws and globalization)...

...Which is enhanced by new technology, and...

...Changing relationships between professionals and the marketers, which leads to...

...Adapting firm structures to better serve both market and firm needs...which leads to...

...New kinds of law and accounting firms, which are more reactive to continuously changing economic and social environments and chaning client needs.

This is the process. Because of the dynamics of events, most of which were unpredictable, the dynamic seems to have a life of its own. There are so many elements involved that are themselves constantly changing that looking at the professions pre-*Bates* – and including the *Bates* decision itself – were unforeseeable, that (to borrow a phrase from Adam Smith), there seems to be an invisible hand at work. However, as we shall see further on, there are techniques to put oneself in rhythm with the process. In fact, it's possible to use the process for more effective planning.

Here's what actually happened…

1. The *Bates* decision struck down the Canons of Ethics and Code of Professional Conduct that prohibited frank marketing – the mandates against frank promotional activities.

2. This engendered a concept only vaguely understood by professionals at the time called competition. The problem at the time was that unlike the commercial world, there was neither history nor tradition in the commonly used marketing techniques. That meant a few years of groping – of trying to find our way to market within the profound limits of the legal and accounting professions, and of learning the differences between marketing a product and marketing a professional service. This is the phase that I call Professional Services Marketing 1.0.

3. But a few firms – both legal and accounting – took the first steps in the competitive battle. Significantly, as others saw that there might be merit in the process, they followed with their own versions of marketing – versions that were relevant to their own markets and their own skills. Thus, the beginnings of the evolutionary process that produced not only change, but irreversible change. At the same time, the economic and social landscape began to change – specifically, globalization, technology, new laws and regulations.

4. Professional services marketing began to settle in as a definable discipline. This accomplished the following…

    a. The market for professional services increased public awareness of the value of the professions, which then increased demands for more sophisticated legal and accounting services. Despite protestations by old-timers that, as one lawyer put it, *Bates* destroyed the profession, *Bates*, in fact, enhanced it, in large measure because marketing educated the market, and in part because one of the ways marketers use to sell its services is to develop new services and new client-oriented techniques in both law and accounting. This second phase in the evolution, in which marketing became more sophisticated, I call Marketing 2.0. That is the phase we are in now – but is still evolving.

b. At the same time, new technology began altering communication between the professional and the media, internally within the firm, and more significantly, between the professionals and the client.

c. As clients became more sophisticated, they demanded more and better service, which began the process of finding ways to increase productivity. Thus began the more intensive use of technology (developing the mobile office, for example).

d. This led to the emergence of new kinds of law and accounting firms, ranging from corporate-like structures to two-tier firms, to out-sourcing (both domestically and abroad), to firms with democratic governance styles. Most significantly, firms that had traditionally been centered on their practice became focused on – and driven by – client needs. An example is the development of the dynamic client service team, so meticulously designed by lawyer/marketer Iris Jones, first at Akin Gump and again at Chadbourne & Parke LLP

e. The competitive process increased the need for more capital than could be supplied by the partners, which is why the subject of public sale of stock is now being floated. It possibly accounts, as well, for the recent rash of professional firm mergers.

5. In the early days following *Bates*, and subsequently well into the current era, the most inhibiting factor impeding effective marketing was the disconnect between the lawyer or the accountant, and the professional marketer. Aside from the lack of marketing tradition in the professions, the professionals showed little understanding of the marketing process and the marketers themselves. Traditionally, there had been little hospitality in the law firm toward the non-lawyer and in the

accounting firm for the non-accountant. This, despite the fact that no other trade or industry demands so much of its members' participation in the marketing effort as does the law and accounting. There are several reasons for this...

a. There is the long-standing tradition that opposes any promotional effort by professionals as undignified, and generally deleterious and demeaning to professional integrity and authority.

b. The education and professionalism of the lawyer and the accountant is extensive and intense. There is usually undergraduate school, graduate school and professional school, followed by apprenticeship, certification, and a long climb to the partnership. Most marketers may have college degrees, and experience in the several disciplines of marketing, but no qualification or apprenticeship to match that of the lawyer or accountant.

c. The anachronistic attempts by state and national bar and accounting societies and associations to protect the integrity of their respective professions. In too many cases, their strictures have failed to take into account the new needs of the professions to compete effectively, using modern techniques. In virtually every case in which the professionals have won rights the societies and the associations have opposed, none of the resulting changes have adversely affected the integrity of the professions.

d. The personality and focus on imagination of the marketer tends to be very different than for the lawyer or accountant. The professional disciplines are too disparate to allow for easy accommodation.

6. This has led to a new relationship between marketers and the professionals they serve, and the emergence of the lawyer/marketer and the accountant/marketer. It's a new partnership in which each member of the team brings skill and experience to the table.

a. This is producing a new sophistication to bear on the competitive environment.

    b. It is a driving force in developing new kinds of firms.

7. The evolving firm is a structure in which…

    a. The client, not the firm, is at the core of the practice.

    b. The concept of value now centers on value to the client – not the firm.

    c. Focus within the firm is on talent, rather than the traditional top-down governance structure.

    d. The legendary (and recently deceased) management consultant Peter Drucker's concept that the purpose of a company is to create a customer is now infiltrating the professional firm.

    e. Technology is now important for more than improving productivity internally, but for improving the ability to serve the client – to the point of further changing the nature of the firm itself, and enhancing the ability to compete.

    f. Where heretofore knowledge management was a process of gathering and retrieving facts, the emphasis now shifts to turning facts into information targeted to enhancing client service, improving marketing, and keeping a firm relevant to the changing needs of its clientele.

    g. New kinds of responsibilities, such as knowledge management, business development, value management, and client retention specialists, are increasingly found in firms – often as specialties.

    h. Client service teams, once merely a collection of the firm's professionals patched together to serve clients, are now more sophisticated and better organized to wrap clients in a blanket of genuine full service.

    i. Client development – the actual selling function – is now considered as distinct from the marketing function, which is the process of developing name recognition, defining skills, and enhancing reputation – all of which are a foundation for the selling function.

These are things that are happening today. Are they universal? No. They are trends – steps in the evolutionary process that ultimately produces change in professional practice and firms, in a delicate balance that not only better serves the client and the firms, but also maintains the traditional concept of professionalism and integrity. And as the late scientist Stephen Jay Gould said, evolution is not a straight line, nor does it happen all at once or universally.

This new phase is creating the foundation of Professional Services Marketing 3.0.

I contend that any professional in that cycle who doesn't react to its dynamics will fall behind those who do.

Inhibitions to Change

This is why I'm puzzled by the law or accounting firm that continues to function today as it did many decades ago – in so many areas, as if the world continues to be as it was decades ago.

At the same time, in the midst of all that's changing in the professional world, I'm surprised that change in the marketing process for professional services is evolving so slowly. There are indeed exceptions, in which a handful of firms have extensive programs that are innovative, and very large staffs to execute them. These few firms have specialists in such activities as business development, media relations, and so forth, but considering the vast number of law and accounting firms, their number is a small percentage of the professions.

There are many reasons for this, not the least of which is the amorphous nature of professional services management and marketing education. The quality of academic and firm marketing education in this field is dismal and retrogressive. The relationship between the marketers and the professional is too often built on mutual misunderstanding. And perhaps it's because law and accounting firm marketing is so subsumed by a firm's professionals with too little understanding of the process, that too many marketers are either unwilling to risk innovation or else are incapable of it.

Perhaps, too, the external factors that require new vision for professionals and their marketers are happening too fast, and are overwhelming both.

And perhaps the traditions and stringent (and sometimes anachronistic) ethical requirements of both law and accounting inhibit innovation.

Still, there are techniques to keep professionals relevant to the changing needs of the clients, and to keep marketing functional and successful beyond the mundane. For example, consider that while the ultimate aim of marketing professional services may be to get clients, growing a successful firm is a function of keeping a firm relevant to the changing nature of its economic and social environment, and particularly the needs of the clientele. Obviously, then the marketer must understand that environment, which then becomes the canvas upon which the marketing program is painted.

This is certainly true in professional services marketing, where recycling old ideas instead of bothering to come up with new ones, is a too common practice, and where the failure of professionals to fully grasp the reality of the crucial role that marketing plays in a practice tends to suppress innovation in so many firms.

It's certainly true in the professions, which are too often inhibited by antiquated traditions, irrational views of ethics in the 21st century, the anachronistic thinking of state and local bar and accounting societies, and a mentality of "We have always lived in the castle."

Possible Changes in The-Not-Too Distant Future

Predicting the future course of events can be a fool's game, especially if the prediction is an extrapolation of current trends and practices. Anticipating future events, by the way, doesn't work well by looking at current practices alone, then – there are too many unpredictable factors.

The reason that predictions are so hard to get right, then, is simple to fathom. In today's dynamic world, any course of action will likely be affected by unforeseeable random events that alter that course. For example, just a few years ago, who could have predicted LinkedIn, or Facebook, or Twitter – much less the impact the social networks would have on society and business? Many of us remember when blogs were considered to be fads that would ultimately die or fade away. Now, blogs are ubiquitous, and an integral part of the business process. The fascinating thing about these devices is that they impacted the business world so rapidly that there wasn't time to predict them before they became important business tools.

What, then, are reasonable assumptions about the future of the legal and accounting professions in this dynamic society? Here, we can surmise – if not predict – a future by extrapolating two things from the past...

- Not as an extension of the past, but a clear view of the dynamics of the process of change itself – its causes and our responses to causes. Change, as we have noted, is not an event – it's an evolutionary process, the *result* of which is change.

- By looking at trends – not just trends in the legal and accounting professions, but rather in the needs of the clients, in the economy, in new law, all of which are evolving rapidly – faster, in fact, than most law and accounting firms are changing. Trends in clients' industries portend changes in the professional firms that serve those clients.

Product manufacturers have an easier time, relatively, than do lawyers or accountants. They use market research to track consumer tastes. They use sales figures to monitor consumer purchasing habits. They have many sources and techniques to analyze and define customer buying practices, particularly for online purchases.

Lawyer's and accountant's clients tend to have distinctive or unique problems, which makes it more difficult – but not impossible – to track and aggregate. Market research, which is too expensive for any but the largest firms, is another way. But at the same time, there is a way to divine trends that can be helpful in long range planning. That way is to track trends in the clients' industries.

That kind of information leads to an understanding of trends in the needs of clients in the near future. And the needs of clients are what define the trend in law and accounting firm management, business planning, governance, and even financial planning.

Why should this work? Because virtually all the changes in professional firm structure and management have come about in response to the needs of effective competition, and the changing demands of clients. The professional services world has been redefined by the ability and the need, to compete –a world opened up by *Bates.*

Technological advances have caused changes in the mechanics of the professions, and will continue to do so. The danger is in believing that the technical advances and the new media are responsible for these changes. Not entirely so. They have facilitated changes, and created new media – but they have not specifically caused change in firm structures and practices. Remember, *Bates* and the ability to compete came well before the internet affected legal and accounting practice. The internet, remember, is simply a new communications structure. What it has done is causing substantial changes in the print media, and caused the development of new techniques for dissemination of information. But the changes in law and accounting firm management are responses to the changing needs and demands of the clientele, to the economy, and to new laws and regulations – and again, the need to compete.

What, then, are the potential areas of change? Some possibilities...

- The fragile partnership structure, which can slow down decision making that should be responsive to changing economic decisions. What will replace it?

- Law and accounting firm billing procedures, which may have a value in informing clients of the time spent in the client's behalf, but rarely reflects the value of the service performed.

- Value billing is emerging, but is still evolving. Who knows for sure which methods will emerge as the standard?

- Partner and non-partner compensation changed radically during the current economic turndown. What will it become as the economy recovers?

- During the course of this recession, thousands of lawyers and accountants were discharged. What will be their availability as the recession recovers? What will be the shape of the accounting and law firms in the recovery? We already see signs of changes in firm structure, in productivity measures, in internal focus on skills rather than status.

- Growth requires capital, which may be more than a firm's partners can contribute. Is the publicly-held law or accounting firm in the foreseeable future? When I suggested this some time ago, a lawyer said to me, "Over my dead body." To which I answered, "Let's talk about all the things that would happen over your dead body – that already have happened." "How do you think it can possibly happen," he asked. "I don't know," I said. "But when the need becomes imminent, you lawyers are very smart. You'll find a way." The same is true, by the way, of corporations owning law and accounting firms, which have already been seen in some iterations.

- The shortage of brains and talent in the world today is too acute to continue the caste system in professional firms. Talented professionals may not be "partner material" (whatever that is). But the need for their skills suggest that in the future, firms may be structured on talent, rather than on traditional methods and requirements like rainmaking abilities and longevity (the two-tier system).

- Today, law and accounting schools send their graduates into the world with little or no education about the economics of practice, nor an understanding of the crucial role modern marketing plays in firm management and growth. Fordham Law School in New York City is having success with courses in law firm management and marketing, promulgated by the marketing expert and educator Silvia Hodges. I've lectured in those courses to a growing attendance. At the same time, the brilliant lawyer and economist Bruce MacEwen is bringing the important subject of law firm economics to an increasing number of law firms. We see signs of change here – but only in isolated incidents to become universal in both professions. That should change – but how?

- In the three decades since *Bates* introduced the concept of frank competition to professional firms, a new and distinctive body of marketing technique has evolved. It has also become clear that professional marketing is integral to the growth of professional firms. Yet today, only the largest of these firms, and a few smaller ones, accept that concept. The sustaining tradition is that only lawyers and accountants have full hospitality in law and accounting firms – despite the well proven efficacy of organized marketing in practice development. How will this disconnect be resolved in the future?

- Despite three decades of experience in professional services marketing, remarkably little innovation seems to have occurred in its practice in recent years. Part of this is because of the random education in professional services marketing in business schools; part because marketing itself is an art form in the way the process is executed – and there are not that many artists. Yet another reason is the lack of formal education in professional services marketing, which is very different from product marketing. A significant factor is that accountants and lawyers have little foundation in how to hire and evaluate marketers, which often results in unsatisfactory marketing process, and failure to judge good from bad – effective from ineffective.

- Because of the disconnect between professionals and marketers, many marketers don't innovate, even in an arena in which all marketers have the same tools. The winners know how to use those tools innovatively; the losers do not. The marketers either feel intimidated by the stature of professionals, or don't know how to do anything except by rote. Perhaps time and competition will temper this situation.

Functioning in a Changing World

While evolution can rarely be accelerated, nor its ultimate destination be accurately foreseen, there may be ways in which it can be accommodated. Accommodation is essential, simply because control of events, when possible, mitigate unpleasant surprise.

Several things beyond outright behavior modification can make it possible for both professionals and marketers to participate in the change process…

- Learn to fathom those elements, both economic and social, that are currently changing. For example, new technology, including the new social media. Even if you don't plan to participate, learn it. You'll understand a great deal of the dynamics of new aspects of society and the economy. You'll spot trends.

- Don't insulate yourself from the marketing process if you're a professional, or from the nature of accounting or law if you're a marketer.

- If you're a marketer, try to understand the lawyer or accountant. This means the people – the lawyers or accountants – as well as the process. The attitudes, the points of view on the clients, the way they think, their values. Don't try to turn them into marketers – marketing is your job – but rather teach them how to be participants in the marketing process. As a marketer, you're not going to change the professionals, but you can educate them within the context of their professions. For example, some years ago, at a major accounting firm, I wondered if an audit could be used as a business management or planning tool. The answer was more arcane than practical, but I learned more about auditing than most non-accountants usually know, and the auditors learned more about marketers and marketing than most of them knew at the time.

- If you're a professional, you don't have to be a marketing professional if you don't want to, but you should know enough about the process to be able to participate in it as appropriate, as well as to understand the marketers and how their minds work. Ultimately, in a successful marketing program, you're going to have to participate in the process and in bringing the prospect into the fold. Learn how to do it well. It's a process well within your training and experience.

- Read the trade media – both the appropriate law and accounting trades and the publications serving the industries the clients are in. Not just for the news, but for the trends.
- When you spot a trend – particularly one that veers from traditional professional practice (such as moving from hourly billing to value billing, or keeping associates or accountants who are talented but not partner material) don't make snap judgments. Not only are these strong trends, but even if you're not ready to bring them into your practice, they may eventually be right for you.

- If you can't innovate, at least learn to respond to external factors that can affect your practice, your firm, and your clients.

- Competitive intelligence is important. You should be aware of other firms and what they're doing that you're not – but should be. Or that may eventually be right for you.

Learn to question everything you do. Ask yourself the question, "This is the way I did it yesterday. Is it the best way to do it today?" You'll be amazed at the answer.

In every aspect of life, there is nothing – not an article, not a process, not an event – that is unaffected by something else. That's why everything you do – large or small – will ultimately change, whether you choose it or not.

Is change a marketing tool? Absolutely, if understanding and dealing with it puts you a step ahead of your competitors. And remember, evolution is constant, and change is coming – whether you participate in it or not. Change is not an option, when the old way is made obsolete by competition.

And so the response to the changing needs of the marketplace, and the need to compete, completely altered the nature of the practice – and continues to do so. In three and a half decades, there has been a substantial evolution. It's a microcosm of the evolutionary cycle. It continues today.

{Chapter 3}

How Marketing Works

Building A Firm – For Now And The Future

To put it simply, professional services marketing is a process that's designed to bring a firm and its prospective clientele together. More than just accumulating clients, the effective marketing program helps shape and secure a practice that's relevant to the dynamic needs of both the firm and the clients it serves. More than a collection of marketing activities, marketing is a process.

The process, essentially, may be perceived in four parts…

1. Define the market

2. Define the service to meet the needs of the market

3. Define the tools of marketing to be used to reach and persuade the market

4. Manage the tools.

The significant body of knowledge about marketing functions in two areas – the techniques, or tools (articles, press releases, collateral material, etc., and they ways they're used), and the study of the markets themselves (such as the demographics, motivation for buying – its shape, its structure, its needs, and its opportunities.). Strategy – the way in which the two are brought together – is crucial. Too much of marketing practice often seems to focus primarily in the tools, rather than in the strategy, which can be a fatal error.

Persuasiveness – Why People Buy

Despite thousands of dollars spent on research about why people choose one professional service firm rather than another, we still know remarkably little. Professional services are, to a large extent, too amorphous to respond to simple motivation, but there are some reasonable surmises that can be made, based on both logic and experience.

Unfortunately, the many home-grown surveys done by law and accounting firms don't go deeply enough into motivations to fully understand how people or firms choose one professional firm over another. Part of the problem resides in the fact that professional services marketing rarely moves people to act immediately, and so the purchase decision is too distant from the marketing effort – unlike product marketing. Part of the problem is that the reasons buyers need or want legal or accounting services are variable and diverse. To a large degree, many individuals – and many companies – make retaining decisions for irrational reasons, such as personal relationships or word of mouth recommendations. In many cases, decisions are made based on reputation or name recognition. Except for larger firms that have either in-house staffs or long-standing relationships with lawyers or accountants, a very large part of the market doesn't have the least idea about how to qualify the professionals they hire. As discouraging as that may sound, it tells us a great deal about how to formulate the elements of a marketing program.

Surveys, moreover, consistently show that how professionals think their clients view their performance and what clients actually think, are usually miles apart.

In other words, experience or not, we know far less than we should know. And so we're back to surmises and objectives.

In the light of what we do know, and considering the singular nature of marketing professional services (as compared, for example, to product marketing), what works? Or more specifically, what seems to work?

- **Name recognition.** Except for corporations and very large or national companies (whose in-house lawyers make the buying decisions), people tend to buy names they recognize. The concept of branding seems to have crept in under the door, but in professional services, branding is simply jargon for name recognition. (Professional services marketers seem to be attracted to jargon, like flies to honey). Stick to the real world and plain English – it works better.) Establishing name recognition, however, is easy – simply inundate the market with your firm's name (see Chapter 22). An ad campaign that says little more than "Smith & Dale is a law firm. We do good work" and saying it over and over again, will give you name recognition, but little more. It helps, but it's not everything.

- **Reputation.** If your firm has a reputation for resolving accounting or legal problems, or for service, or for not overcharging, or for anything good, it goes to building trust – which is an essential element in professional services. Trust is an essential factor in retaining professionals.

- **Specialty.** If your firm has a reputation in a specialty – estate planning, labor relations, cash flow management, etc., it's a major factor in being considered by a prospective client.

- **Demonstrating expertise.** A significant reason you are asked to propose is that your reputation is founded on demonstrable expertise. This is accomplished by such activities as writing articles, social media, speaking, participating in seminars, public relations, and other such devices.

- **Networking.** In the old days, it was the golf course or the country club. Today, it's done by planned participation in organizations in the fields served by your prospective clients. Case history – A client of mine belonged to an organization of business people. Her specialty was labor law. The problem was that another member, who was also a labor lawyer and a competitor, was running seminars for the organization's members. Our plan was for the client to become visible and active in the organization, volunteering, offering to run for office, and so forth. We then came up with a specific seminar idea that hadn't been done before. It worked. Harry Potter and his wand couldn't have done it better.

- **Client referrals and word of mouth.** Clients who are particularly satisfied with your work will enthusiastically recommend you to other prospective clients. Your clients may have to be prompted, but it's worth the effort. Word of mouth (now called by the peculiar name, *viral marketing – more jargon*), in which people tell one another about your virtues, is a marvelous concept, but difficult to generate. You have to do something worth talking about, though (my accountant saved me thousands of dollars, etc...). Viral marketing will, in the long run, sell more beer or tomato soup than it will legal or accounting services.

- **Influentials.** In both accounting and law, there are always people from other professions or trades who are in a position to recommend you. Not just lawyers who recommend accountants, or vice-versa, but bankers, business leaders, relatives and friends. A client once told me that if he could take a banker to lunch once a week, he'd double his practice in a year. A colleague asked, "But what do I talk about? Our firm?" No, you talk about his or her business and clients. You listen. And if you listen carefully, you're going to hear something to which you can say, "We can help with that. Can you arrange an appointment?" It works.

- **Serendipity.** Or luck, is more like it. A lawyer for a former client of mine claimed that he brought in clients by hanging out in a bar and conversing with strangers. And he did both. Everybody has a story, and if you're lucky, and listen, and play it right, you can do it to. However, serendipity is great, but you can't build much of a practice on it.

- **Practice development.** At some time in every marketing campaign, the name recognition and reputation and networking come to a point at which the prospect has to agree to start Monday. This may require some heavy-duty work, which is how the concept of practice development comes into play. The prospect must be sold. A request for a proposal may have to be answered. The prospect may be considering other of your competitors. This goes well beyond the skills of name recognition and reputation building, which is why the specialty of practice development evolved.

Because a professional services marketing program must do more than accumulate clients, and because it must function in a dynamic world that's constantly in flux, an effective marketing program can't be a static list of activities that use a static list of marketing tools. It must have clear objectives that are flexible enough to accommodate the dynamic nature of the market. It must focus specific aspects of a practice, predicated on the distinctive needs of each aspect of the prospective clientele. For example, a marketing program to attract high asset individuals is different from one to attract corporations. A program to attract real estate developers is different than one to attract builders.

And while it's commonly assumed that the idea is to sell the firm, experience shows that marketing professional services works best when it focuses on individual market segments. A program that does that well results in projecting a capable firm in all its parts. Obviously, then, a clear understanding of each market served is essential.

In other words, no one size marketing program fits all. How, then, recognizing the foregoing differences, can marketing programs be devised that are focused, effective, and competitive?

The answer resides in formulating objectives for each program, based on the distinctive characteristics of each market.

SETTING OBJECTIVES

If you don't know where you're going, how do you know how to get there? Absent clear goals, marketing efforts become random, diverse and expensive. With clearly delineated objectives, marketing programs and marketing activities become relevant and focused. They offer a test against which all activities are measured. If a marketing activity doesn't clearly serve to meet a specific objective, it's usually wasteful, inept, and not cost-effective.

Two things about planning that are immutable…

- Firm and marketing plans are intertwined. As the old song goes, you can't have one without the other. The objectives for the firm and the objectives for the marketing program must closely relate to one another, simply because no serious firm plan can be viable without the marketing thrust to make it so, nor can any marketing program be effective if it's not relevant to the firm plan.

- Both plans begin with a realistic assessment of the market to be served, and with an understanding of the skills necessary to reach and serve the market.

It's important that objectives be realistic and achievable, and not just wishful thinking. Setting objectives, then, even for the smallest firms, is not an abstract exercise. And therefore, all firm plans and their objectives must begin with a clear understanding of the market to be served. *Not to recognize this is to court meaningless and irrelevancy in all planning.*

Firm Objectives

Practically, a firm's plan should be in two parts – near-term and long-term. Near-term should be no longer than two or three years. Beyond that, there are too many variables in the economy, in law, in regulations, etc. to be valid – even with the flexibility that should be part of any plan. Longer than that, it becomes a wish list – not to be ignored, but seen for what it is – a long-term goal. The short-term goal, on the other hand, should be action-oriented, with an action plan for each goal, including who does it.

Within the context of the market and the firm's skills, there then follows a readily defined understanding of what the firm and its partners want, both in the near and the far term, and what they hope to have the marketing program and action plan accomplish in pursuit of those goals. An overriding consideration is your decision as to the nature of your practice. What are your growth parameters? How do you mean the firm to serve the personal and professional needs of you and your partners (and not to be overlooked, your staff)? How do you want to be perceived by your clientele? What skills do you have that are marketable and which do you need to acquire? How? What will you demand of your partners and staff? Do you mean to change the firm's structure or form of governance to be more responsive to the needs of your market? Do you foresee changing from hourly to value billing? What are your target dates, and what is your budget?

Perspective is important. In all cases, the objective may be to recast a firm to be more relevant to the changing social and economic environment. Objectives, clearly defined as they should be, should not be overwhelming. Nor should they be adhered to slavishly. It's often enough to know what you want to do, why you want to do it, and how you plan to get it done.

And as Gerald A. Riskin and Patrick J. McKenna remind us in their excellent book, *Practice Development*, objectives should be consistent with a firm's comfort level, and should certainly be ethically acceptable to both the firm and the profession practiced by the firm.

Specific Factors

In defining firm objectives, some specific factors must be considered:

Firm Environment. Nothing – not even profitability – is more important than the kind of firm you are or want to be. Without a firm environment that's satisfying and fulfilling to its partners and staff, there will be no growth, no profitability, no future.

Size. Businesses usually don't grow substantially by accident. It's almost invariably a conscious decision by its partners or owners, who then take steps to implement that decision. However, some professional firms may feel that they want to limit their growth, fully cognizant of the implications of growing and managing a large firm. Growth alone may not be of the essence – even a firm that chooses to stay at its current size must make that a conscious decision. But it should face the fact that in order to contain growth, it must take steps to sustain its size; it must perform marketing functions to overcome loss by attrition.

Profitability. Profitability, of course, is as much a function of margins as it is of volume, and so it's useful to know your costs as precisely as possible – a particularly difficult task in a professional firm, particularly because legal and accounting practices are intellectual products, which are difficult to measure. Profitability becomes, as well, a function of the kind of service you're offering, and the kind of market you want to reach.

Corporate work, for example, may have higher margins than working for not-for-profit organizations.

Time Frame. The ability of a car to accelerate – to go from zero to a hundred miles an hour – is measured in seconds. The ability of a firm to meet its firm objectives is measured in a larger time frame. But two things are necessary. First there must be a time frame for the objectives to be met, and second, that time frame must be realistic.

It can, however be flexible. It can allow, for example, five years for the firm to double in size, if that's what it wants, but only two years to expand its market geographically.

Pricing. Pricing is as much an element of marketing as is advertising or promotion. Aside from the fact that it affects revenues and profitability, it also affects positioning. The classic question, for example, is do I charge less and go for volume, or do I charge more and go for a more affluent clientele? This is a function of conscious choice, although often, the choice is dictated by such other factors as access to affluent clients, the ability to supply the kind of service needed, or in some cases, simply the ability to ask for and sustain a high fee schedule. Value billing is on its way to superseding hourly billing, which raises the complex question of defining *value*. But the consideration is value to the client before value to the firm – or there will quickly be no value to the firm.

Not to be overlooked is that in today's competitive climate, pricing has become a tool of marketing, in ways that it had not been before. As in other forms of marketing, pricing is sometimes set by competition, where before it had been relatively arbitrary. A price war, however tends to ignore value, and is often disastrous.

Market. There are three aspects of a market that must be considered – its size, its needs, and its location – and all three must be viewed carefully in formulating objectives. How large a market can you realistically serve? What are the parameters of the market's needs that you're prepared to serve effectively? What geographical limitations are realistic? Do we have the skills to succeed in a particular market?

Share of Market. When a firm is in a rapidly growing market, or functioning in an era of rapid growth, share of market is not significant. Growth will come with the market. But when that market or industry slows its growth, and competition for existing business is the only possibility for growth, then share of market is crucial. If the only way to grow is to capture your competitor's clients, then obviously, your share of market grows as your competitor's diminishes.

Share of market is an equally important consideration in an industrially mature market area, where industry is either stagnating or declining, and where a substantial part of a practice is in the mature industry.

Still, within those strictures that dictate strong competition or static markets, growth can come by offering new services to existing clients, or by offering new services to clients of other firms. If market share is meaningful, it's measured not only in terms of the total practice, but for specific services as well. A major accounting firm, for example, may be only the fifth largest firm in town, but it may have 70% of the market in small business services.

And of course, the two classic approaches to increasing market share are price cutting, which is now more complex than merely lowering prices, and is therefore fraught with danger, and improved marketing efforts, which is infinitely preferable.

Service Concept. As a professional service, your relations with your clients dictate that they are served personally. One major accounting firm opened a second office in the Wall Street area of New York, ostensibly to serve the needs of its financial clients (and to expand its financial clientele.) Another accounting firm opened a branch office in suburban Dallas, to better serve the growing number of smaller businesses located there. The service option, of course, is the firm's, but it should be made a specific choice. If it's not, if it's arrived at arbitrarily, it sends a diverse message to clients, and is counterproductive to a firm's growth and success.

But in the final analysis, the tools and strategies of marketing serve to enhance the practice development process.

It's always wise, also, to consider those elements that are beyond individual control. One can't control, for example, the economy, which can throw the best formulated objectives awry. An entire legal practice can be created or destroyed by a legislative change. An accounting practice can be made or broken by a new tax law, or a new FASB change. Opportunities for professionals are generated or obliterated regularly. This is why objectives are never more than guidelines that serve to define a course of action, whether in marketing or otherwise.

There's always the danger, too, of successfully achieving marketing objectives too soon, and thereby outrunning your ability to serve a new or growing clientele. It makes little sense to do a successful job of increasing your tax business if you can't find a sufficient number of tax specialists to serve your new clientele.

FORMULATING MARKETING OBJECTIVES

Firm objectives are the context for marketing programs, which are, in turn, the blueprints for achieving firm objectives. To think of marketing otherwise is to court marketing programs that are irrelevant and unproductive.

The word *market* warrants some clear definition. A market is a group, of any size, with a common need or purpose. A market is a group that can be reached by common media. A market group is dynamic, subject to change, to reorganize, to respond to such external forces as the economy, law and regulation, and social factors.

Recognizing that the shape of any market group is at best amorphous, the prudent marketer must be dedicated to understanding each market group's dynamic, its immediate as well as its potential needs, and the factors that affect its foundation. For example, significant financial regulation changes the nature of the financial market for both accountants and lawyers. New laws and regulations, changes in accounting principles or tax laws – all affect the nature of the market. And all generate new marketing activities. Not every company in a market is right for your firm, but fortunately, the electronic media makes it possible to do two things that help – learn a great deal about most target companies, and tailor specific marketing efforts to a particular company. It's called target marketing, obviously.

Publics. In any market there are several publics. There are existing clients, whose needs for service must be constantly addressed, as must be their needs for new services. There are the prospective clients, who constitute as many publics as there are services you can perform for them. Your firm may serve one public with corporate services, another in the same market group with financial services, and a third in the same market with personal financial services. The three groups may be contiguous, but each may still be separate and distinct.

Defining a target audience is a function of determining those universal characteristics of the target group to which your services are most profitably addressed. The universal characteristics must include the ability to reach them in a uniform and economical way.

An effective marketing program can have rather specific goals, beyond getting new clients. For example:

- To build a practice with substantive clients

- To increase market share or a presence in a new market

- To broaden a geographic base

- To introduce a new service

- To change the structure of the clientele and the nature of the firm

- To change a perception of a firm by its market

- To enter a new market for a specific service

- To sell new services to existing clients, as well as to new clients

- To strengthen relationships with existing clients

But within the context of these goals, the key elements to examine in setting marketing objectives are...

- To enhance name recognition and reinforce reputation

- To demonstrate the firm's skills and capabilities, particularly specific to each market

- To develop positions in new markets and enhance positions in existing markets

- To develop the opportunities to meet with prospects in a selling context

Client Perception. How do you want to be perceived by your clientele? While the answer to that question is crucial to the marketing plan, it should be remembered that marketing cannot develop images – a perception that too often belies reality. No marketing program can convey an image of high service at low cost if, in fact, you are not performing high service at low cost. The acoustics of the marketplace are extraordinary, and as Ralph Waldo Emerson said, what you are speaks so loudly that people can't hear what you say you are.

It's easier to project a negative perception of your firm than a positive one. For example, advertising and other promotional material that attempt to be funny but aren't don't do much to define a serious firm.

If your objective is to change the way you're perceived, then you must first change what's necessary to make the way you want to be perceived a reality. Then, and only then, can you expect a marketing program to project those elements that will contribute to a realistic perception of your firm, and to a reputation that serves your marketing goals.

Time Frame. A practical and realistic time frame in which to achieve specific goals is essential to establishing marketing objectives. Marketing must be given a reasonable time to work. And yet, if it's not working within a reasonable time, this should be recognized in time to make adjustments. Unreasonable expectations are a clear danger, in terms of both results and time frame. Marketing professional services has a longer time frame than does product marketing. A retailer placing an ad knows his results almost immediately, by the number of people who come into the store. In professional services, the results are felt not when the brochure or direct mail piece goes out, or the release is printed or the ad is run, but when the contracts are signed.

Revenues and Return on Investment. Presumably, the objective is to increase revenues by increasing the clientele or the services to existing clients. But at what cost? In designing a marketing program, the cost of achieving a revenue goal – the return on investment – is a primary factor.

Merely to set an arbitrary figure or percentage increase is insufficient, without asking pertinent questions about what must be spent to achieve that goal. Nor is the expenditure in marketing dollars alone. The increased revenue, presumably from increased volume, must be serviced. Will new staff have to be added? How much will new staff add to overhead, in both salaries and support costs – space, secretarial and clerical help, support services, and so forth?

Thus, in setting a goal for increased revenues, the size of the investment to achieve that increase must be calculated, and from that must be determined the goal for return on that investment.

It must also be recognized, in this context, that in marketing, there is rarely a one-to-one relationship between efforts and results. An ad that costs a hundred dollars cannot be expected to produce two hundred dollars in revenue the week after it's run. Marketing has a dynamic, particularly if it's successful. A well-run campaign increases in effectiveness as it continues, and as the effectiveness increases, so does the return on investment. For example, an accounting firm may identify a need for a new service to banks. The firm must spend a certain amount of money to develop that service, and then to make it known to its prospective clientele. At the beginning, it's talking to a market that may be as unaware of the firm as it is of the service. But after a period of sustained marketing effort, the market is educated, and it takes less to sell more.

It should be noted, however, that the converse is not necessarily true. If the effort is diminished, there is no sustaining recollection by the market. Other competitors move in, and the value of the earlier efforts are lost. It's like a hoop. As long as you keep hitting it with a stick, it keeps rolling, picking up momentum. But when you stop hitting the hoop, it falls over. It doesn't matter how far it's rolled or where it's been. It's down and out.

At the beginning of a marketing campaign, the return on the investment is smaller. But if the investment and the effort is sustained, the penetration of the effort is greater for the same dollar, and so the return on investment is greater.

Budget. There are a number of techniques for determining budgets. But it's not a simple process, and requires a great deal of consideration. And again, it should be remembered that in budgeting, effectiveness – and therefore return on investment – will increase as the marketing program gains in penetration.

Share of Market. If share of market is a significant element in your growth or competitive picture, then it must be generally quantified, and marketing plans must reflect the competitive values in your efforts.

THE MARKETING PROGRAM

The tools of marketing are not a program – they are simply tools.

A marketing program, then, is not simply a catalogue of tools. It's a plan – a strategy and a tactical plan. It's the sum total of all relevant activities, supporting one another, and not just random activities designed without objective, nor relevance to the needs of the prospective client.

It begins with a realistic understanding of the needs and opportunities of the markets you serve. It defines your abilities to meet those needs. It develops a strategy to persuade your market that you can serve its needs. And it formulates the tactics needed to make that strategy functional.

By defining the target audience first, you can devise the strategy to address that audience, by…

- Defining the needs and opportunities of that market segment

- Designing collateral material addressed to that audience

- Writing articles and developing other media activities for media that serves that market.
- Networking through organizations that serve that market
- Running seminars for companies in that segment

- Doing specialized newsletters

- Using the social media effectively

- Using carefully targeted direct mail

There is an important difference between telling a target audience what you want them to think ("We have great skills, so hire us"), and leading that audience to that conclusion on its own. ("Our real estate partners not only have three decades of experience, but..."). The first statement may gratify your ego, but it's self-serving and has no credibility. The second statement gives a reason to consider – and maybe trust –the firm, and says a lot about the firm itself.

The major strategy should be to market practice by practice, and service by service.

You can't say, "We have great skills, so hire us." That kind of statement doesn't distinguish you from your competitors, nor is it credible. You can't say, "We believe in client satisfaction" for the same reasons. And that's why you can't expect any strategy to market your skills and ability to serve clients by marketing the entire firm. Each practice, each skill set, should have its own marketing program.

Positioning

Positioning is one of the most important aspects of a marketing program (see Chapter 7). It defines in the greatest detail possible what the prospective clientele most needs, demonstrates that you understand those needs, and explains why you're most capable of serving those needs. The position thus defined becomes the thrust of your marketing program. It focuses your marketing program like a laser beam.

Realities to Consider

In formulating marketing objectives, as in firm objectives, there are some basic realities to consider, such as...

- How realistic are the objectives? Can they be achieved as marketing objectives? Is the market really there for what you want to offer? Can the firm really deliver what it plans to market?

- Does the firm really understand the cost of meeting those marketing objectives, in terms of staff? Dollars available? Professional staff time? Risk of failing in any particular marketing effort or activity?

- Has the firm realistically assessed its commitment to marketing, in terms of supporting the creative effort, the staff, and the program?

Not facing these realities, and not understanding what's involved in moving into the marketing arena, can be wasteful and expensive.

And the major objective of the well designed marketing program?

To get the opportunity to meet the prospect face to face, in order to sell. The ultimate objective, and the only ultimate objective, is to get the client.

When the marketing objectives are clear, then there can be a clear view of the program itself. Only then can there be a valid assessment of the marketing mix – those several tools of marketing that, together, move the program forward, and the blueprint to accomplish it.

But professional services offer a different environment, than does product marketing, defined both in the nature of the professional service and in the way that service is delivered. Moreover, generations of tradition in the professions have shifted the focus from the customer – the client – to the professional, in large measure for artificial – if sustaining – reasons. Rarely can a consumer of professional services be persuaded of the need for a professional until the need for a professional's services emerge. One is sued. An audit is demanded of a company by either the government or a source of finance. One needs a contract to seal an agreement.

And this, then, is the element that drives the singular nature of marketing professional services – the constantly changing relationship between the professional and the client. It is tempered not by a manufacturing process, but by changing personalities, changing circumstances, changing laws and regulations beyond the control of either professionals or clients, the infusion of new and different economic or social elements. It is further complicated by the fact that in today's dynamic economy, where all commerce is affected by new technology, new interplays, new relationships and new intercultural demands, the relationship between the client and the professional is rarely the same from one day to the next. Nor are tomorrow's demands of the professional likely to be satisfied by yesterday's solutions.

The Tools

Is advertising part of it? How will public relations fit in? What about publications – newsletters, brochures, etc.. How will the social media be used? What's the role of networking? And so on.

The tools of marketing – public relations, publications, social media, brochures and web sites, networking – are finite. Even as they change (the role of the internet and social media to diminish the hard copy press, for example) they are available to everybody. Which means that the better competitor is the one who uses the tools most imaginatively, most relevantly to the needs of his or her market, most effectively.

The skills of a competent marketer are multifarious. He or she must be a market planner, a writer in several media, a public relations expert, knowledgeable about advertising and the social media, and in a larger firm, a good manager. In view of the relative newness of marketing for the professions, the competent marketer must have the skills to educate the firm and communicate internally as well as externally. The competent marketer must know how to hire not only staff, but outside suppliers, such as public relations firms, art directors, and advertising agencies. Above all, the professional marketer is imaginative in using the tools, without which the program is simple mechanics, and not competitive.

Selling, of all parts of marketing, has always been an integral part of the process, but never until recently has the word or concept of selling been popular in the professional's lexicon. To most professionals, it has always been inimical to the loftiness of professional practice. "If my mother wanted me to be a salesman she wouldn't have sent me to law or accounting school," was a commonly heard statement in the early days of marketing. But ultimately, it must be recognized that all the marketing effort in the world for professional services will rarely – rarely – produce a client. It can only produce a receptive prospect. The prospect buys only when a lawyer or accountant makes the sale, face to face. While this has always been the case, selling is only recently recognized as a part of marketing, albeit a separate skill. Now known as practice development, the practice itself has been pioneered by such thoughtful and experienced marketers as Silvia Coulter and Suzanne Lowe, through both their excellent writing and well-attended conferences and seminars.

Practice Development recognizes that the marketing program is the backdrop for actually producing a client. It goes beyond the marketing program, then beyond the standard selling techniques, by dwelling heavily on understanding complex client needs, listening carefully to client concerns, and relating appropriate firm services to prospective client needs. It's distinctive now because the concept of selling, in professional services, has for so long been anathema to the professions. It's acceptable now because it's rooted in relationship with need, and predicated on solving client problems, and goes well beyond merely hawking firm services.

The tools, then, must be managed. The public relations and direct mail and networking and other efforts must be put into play, in a proper framework, so that they are effective and relevant to the objectives.

This is marketing. It's how a practice is built and shaped, by both sole practitioners and multinational firms.

Tactics

Tactics are the most difficult part of a professional firm marketing program, because so much of what must be done depends upon the scarce, non-billable time of partners and professional staff. If the firm management hasn't made clear that participation by every professional in the firm is an integral part of recognition and growth within the firm, you can scrap the marketing program. It can be helpful if the non-billable hour was renamed the investment hour, because if those hours are spent on marketing, investment hours are exactly what they are.

The marketing professional can do a great deal. He or she may be able to write an article or a brochure, but needs the input of the practitioner. The marketing professional may be able to design and run a seminar, or arrange for a speech, but the practitioner must supply the content. The marketing professional may be able to place the story in the media, but the practitioner must supply the story.

And all of these activities must be managed. They must be prioritized.

They must be made to happen, whether at the behest of a marketing professional or a partner in charge of marketing. They must be timed, and coordinated.

Expectations

Delineating expectations, as part of defining objectives, serves another purpose, albeit one just as useful.

If the prospect doesn't have vast experience in marketing, or in any of its parts, it has no way of knowing what to expect from marketing efforts. Why shouldn't anyone expect a rush of clients, for example, from a single ad – unless that person has been educated very specifically in what an ad can and can't do? Why shouldn't a marketing campaign produce a rapid return of inquires from a well-developed ad campaign?

There are too many cases of partners expecting that press releases will be printed verbatim, that interviews will be reported accurately, that a three-day sales training course will double the size of the clientele within weeks. This is why expectations must be precisely delineated, and why marketers must be educators.

What you should expect from an effective marketing campaign is…

- Name recognition.

- That a great deal is known about your firm and its capabilities.

- That the market will view your firm favorably and will retain a sufficient measure of the campaign's message to remember the firm when the need for its services arises,

- That the market will identify a problem or a need that it has or expects to have, within the context of your firm's capabilities and skills.

- That the market will believe that your firm has the capability to understand and solve the problem.
- That some action, such as an inquiry, be taken (if appropriate), or that the reader be receptive to a follow up call.

Measuring marketing results is one of the discipline's thorniest problems.

There is simply no tangible measure that offers any valuable information that goes beyond the pragmatic or subjective.

The best that can be expected of it is to serve as a red carpet to develop a personal meeting. It does it by pre-selling; by educating; by whetting the appetite for a solution to a problem that you've identified and understand. But don't expect anybody to call and say "I liked your letter (or ad, or blog). Start Monday."

In other words, the expectations are tempered by the quality of the way in which the medium is used. Poor advertising, poor public relations, poor direct mail – all mean sharply diminished performance. To ask more than the medium is capable of producing, or that level of quality can deliver, is a vast self-deception.

Professional Services Marketing 3.0

The emerging relationship between professional and client, and between the marketers and the professionals, is further complicated by the changing nature of the professions themselves, in which several phenomena are redefining the nature of the professions.

In planning for both a firm and its marketing program, there are three factors that should be understood.

- The nature of the professional firm, static for so many generations, is undergoing radical change. This process is influenced by a vast array of factors, many of which are new, some of which are unforeseeable.

- Where once professionals were isolated from marketers and marketing, they are now becoming active participants in the process, and many of them – lawyers and accountants – are themselves becoming astute marketers.

- The driving force of this evolutionary process is the need to compete, imaginatively, and innovatively. It's enhance and accelerated by technology, which itself is in a constant state of innovation and flux.

These factors, then, add up to the reality that if accountants and lawyers are to compete successfully in today's marketplace – if they are to function successfully in the changing arena of professional services, there must be a shift in emphasis from the tenets of the old marketing to the realities of the new. They must accept the significance of relationships as an element of marketing that makes marketing professional services different from marketing products.

How does this translate into practice? What must be done to the strategic 3.0 plan to assure the professional firm survival in the coming decades?

It starts not with a radical redesign of the traditional firm – that will come of itself – but with assessment that springs from the old and goes to the new. It will not be imposed – it will emerge. For example…

- All marketing, old and new, begins with the market itself. It begins to dawn on today's professional that the heart of the practice is not the lawyer or accountant, but the client. Gone is the day of the lawyer or accountant who tells, but doesn't listen. Today and tomorrow, a professional is not an existential entity – he or she is only as he or she does.

- This is further exacerbated by recognizing that a view of the marketplace may begin with history, but must end in the future. Not where the market has been in the demand and need for services, but where it is going to be tomorrow. There are new rhythms in the marketplace, and the professional must be prepared to hear them, and then dance to them.

- The professional – the lawyer or the accountant – must reassess his or her own ability to shift the focus of thinking from the past to the future. There must be a willingness to free oneself from the shackles of the past. While the body of law, or the principles of accounting, remain the bulwarks of the segments of society they govern, they are, first of all, not entirely inflexible, nor are their uses and devices immune from innovative use. *It is this very flexibility that is making possible the figurative osmosis on both sides of the membrane that separates law and accounting.* The answer, then, is not to fight it, but to find ways to use it.

  The sticking factor here is the need that both commerce and society continue to have for the objectivity, the independence, the probity of the professional. *But change need not put these factors in jeopardy.* Rather, the professions can readily find ways to innovate without losing these important virtues.

What must also be re-examined is the structure of the professional firm itself. No longer is the traditional hierarchical structure of the professional firm adequate to the needs of the contemporary marketplace. The range of management skills needed to run the contemporary firm have outgrown traditional structures. The partnership structure tends not to make the best uses of management skills, and impedes the pace at which management decisions must be made. The practice group structure, with certain safeguards built in, seems a likely structural path for the near term, but may not be adequate in the long term, as economic changes compound.

- The professional firm must now be recognized for what it is – a structure to deal with the market it serves. It must recognize that it no longer exists for itself, but *as an instrument to get and sustain clients.* Lawyering or accounting is merely the services provided to fill the channels opened by the devices of marketing. A full and comfortable room in the house must be opened for the professional marketer. At the same time, the professional marketer must know more than traditional marketing, if he or she is to adequately serve the professional. The marketer must understand the lawyer or the accountant, and in ways that surpass the traditional understanding of product. In other words, what had been an us-and-them relationship becomes a marketer/professional partnership.

- It is astonishing that every lawyer, and every accountant, knows that livelihood and career growth depend upon the ability to deliver and keep clients. And yet, as we enter the millennium, there is virtually no law school or accounting school that recognizes that there are skills the professional must know to survive. But sink or swim is no longer a viable preparation for any professional. The elitism of professionals festers at professionals' schools, and must be routed out, if the professional is to thrive in the coming decades. As of this writing, Fordham Law School is giving courses, taught by Silvia Hodges, on law firm management and marketing. There are now others. This could be the beginning of a valuable trend.

- Continuing professional education is no longer a service to the professions alone –it is an obligation to those served by professionals. Nor should it be limited to only the skills of the profession. There is too much to be known about commerce and industry and the needs of clients in a dynamic economy. *There are too many skills that professionals need to know that they don't know.*

- The management skills needed to run a professional firm are a different set of skills than those that are needed to merely sit at the head of a firm. A professional firm is a business. A professional firm that competes is a marketing entity. There are new problems in motivation, in hierarchical structuring, in strategic planning, in human resources management, in client relationships, and in relationships to a new market. The demands of this new kind of management bring the skills of management to a new realm of artfulness – one for which the traditional lawyer or accountant is rarely trained.

- And the ultimate lesson to be learned is that the catalytic element of tomorrow's professional services marketing is that the relationship that begins with the market – the client – now includes the professional. As one moves and changes, so too must the other.

The tools of marketing are, of themselves, immutable. Except perhaps for the use of the internet, nothing much has changed in generations. We still have networking, and public relations and speeches and seminars and articles. We still understand the need for fathoming the markets we serve, and the strategy for using the tools to reach that market. But the difficult lesson to learn is that the value of the tools is not in themselves, but in how innovatively, persuasively, imaginatively they are used.

But it is only when we understand the changing relationships between the professional and the client, and the need to nurture ones ability to function in that relationship with flexibility and agility, that the professions will be able to adapt and survive the coming generations.

That is Professional Services Marketing 3.0.

{Chapter 4}

Building A Marketing Culture
Moving Into Professional Services Marketing 3.0

How do a firm and its people become part of Professional Services Marketing 3.0?

Part of the answer resides in building a marketing culture within a firm, which means that everyone in the firm understands that he or she has an active role in marketing and practice development and understand what that role entails.

It means that professionals have an attitude that grants enthusiastic hospitality to marketing.

Firms may have their *rainmakers* – the partner who could go into a revolving door alone and come out arm in arm with a new client – but in today's competitive marketplace, one or two rainmakers are not enough – if only because the competitive firms have three or more rainmakers going after the same prospective clients that you want. The firms that want to grow and thrive must be turned into marketing machines – to have a culture that understands and supports a marketing effort.

Defining a Marketing Culture
A firm may be said to have a marketing culture when it's professional staff...

- Understands and recognizes the role that marketing plays in firm management and development.

- Understands and respects the professionalism of the marketing professional and the marketing staff.

- Recognizes the relationship between what they do and the needs of the marketplace.

- Understands and accepts its role in the marketing process.

- Understands and accepts that non-billable hours spent on marketing are an investment in the future of the firm, and are not simply non-billable hours.

- Participates in specific marketing activities.

- Retains and supports competent professional marketing staff.

- Structures the firm to develop and pursue a marketing program.

- And ultimately, is managed by people who understand and enthusiastically support the marketing effort.

A firm that meets these criteria is one that will compete successfully, function profitably, and grow.

Building a Marketing Culture

Building a marketing culture is a process that requires…

- Top management support

- Good marketing professionals

- Marketing education of appropriate firm professionals

- A sound and professional marketing structure within the firm

Management Support

Merely to have the managing partner say, "OK, let's do it" is not enough. Whatever the management style – lead by example, exhort, mandate – it's not the same thing as being able to understand and then explain why marketing activities are essential for the growth of the firm; that people will be rewarded for marketing activities; that a measure of non-billable hours applied to marketing is not only acceptable but cherished; that marketing activity is a factor that contributes to measuring partners, associates, and other professional staff compensation. Top management support means inculcating into the firm the concept that in all professional activities, the client is at the core. Top management support means more than acceptance of marketing – it means leadership.

Good Marketing Professionals

Someone once said that if you're smart enough to be a lawyer or an accountant, you're smart enough to do your own marketing. Sure. And you're probably smart enough to be a nuclear physicist – but that doesn't make you one.

Marketing may not be nuclear physics, but it is a profession with its own practices, experiences, skills, and techniques. The good marketing professional is trained in the tools and mechanics of marketing, in its ideas and concepts, in its highly focused point of view. Experience tells the marketing professional what may work and what may not work. If the marketer is imaginative and deft in using imagination, you get a program that's thoughtful and specifically relevant to your needs. And the good marketer understands your profession and its needs.

The good marketer understands the distinctive nature of lawyers and accountants, and is capable of working well with them. He or she has more than a passing understanding of the legal or accounting profession – how it functions, how it serves clients, how the firm is structured, and the professional wishes of the partners and staff. And understands as well the character and personality of the lawyer or the accountant. As a professional, the good marketer belongs to, and is active in, the association of law (LMA – *Legal Marketers Association*) or accounting firm marketers (AAM – *Association of Accounting Marketers*), benefiting from the experience of peers, and contributing as well.

The good marketing professional is also a teacher, who knows how to impart the meaning and techniques of marketing skills to lawyers' and accountants who are not themselves trained marketers. The good marketer is a leader, capable of leading professionals in marketing activities and concepts, and of managing marketing staff. As a communicator, the marketer must establish and maintain a good working relationship with the partners and staff, and keep them informed of marketing activities and aware of each professional's responsibilities in the marketing program.

Remember, the tools of marketing are available to everyone. What counts, then, is the experience and imagination the marketer brings to those skills. It's more than the sum of the skills and mechanics, it's the artistry with which they're used. When you're hiring a marketing professional, then, don't hire the mechanic – hire the artist.

The Professional's Role

The marketing professional can build the marketing program that enhances name recognition and reputation, and that can project the lawyer or accountants' skills and special capabilities, but ultimately, the client has to meet the person or people who are going to perform the legal or accounting service. The bond between client and practitioner – the trust needed in a professional relationship – is a personal relationship that no salesperson can engender for a professional.

But the marketing activities that the lawyer or accountant can do, particularly under the aegis of the marketing professional, are essential. For example…

- The professional – the lawyer or accountant – with the marketer's help, can write articles, can participate in seminars, can make speeches.

- Under the marketer's guidance, the professional can improve networking skills, particularly under a carefully devised networking program.

- The professional can learn to contribute to such marketing activities as writing articles for a firm or firm practice newsletter or blog.

- The professional can learn how to follow up a contact made by direct mail, or by attending firm seminars and networking afterwards.

- While the professional who is not an instinctive sales person is not likely to become one, any intelligent professional can learn the selling skills necessary to convert a prospect into a client. The process is a relatively simple business transaction.

- A professional can learn how to keep a client, once the client is in the house.

- A professional can learn to understand the broader marketing program, and his or her role in it, without having to become a professional marketer.

These are things that merely broaden individual intelligence and education for the lawyer or accountant at no cost to professionalism.

When a firm's professionals participate in these activities, and each participant accepts responsibility for performance, you have three things – involvement, motivation – and a firm marketing culture.

The Practice Group

While there are many approaches to structuring a firm for marketing and improving client service, perhaps the most successful, as defined by Patrick McKenna and David Maister in their masterful book, *First Among Equals*, is the practice group. For any firm with more than a few lawyers or professionals, the practice group is proving to be the most effective way to manage a practice. It recognizes that each practice area has a different target audience. The practice group allows the professionals in that group to address the specific practice and marketing problems of the practice, and to manage them effectively. Among the advantages of the practice group are…

- It's defined by a specific practice within a firm, or a specific target audience. It could be a real estate group, or a tax practice, or a group offering computer services – anything defined by a discrete practice or market that's served by professionals within the firm. The advantages are that every member of the group shares a common set of skills with the others in the group, addresses a common market, and most significantly, has the intellectual capability to help develop a distinctive marketing program to attract that market.

- It can enhance the skills of its members.

- It can share the burden of a marketing effort. For example, if the group publishes brochures, newsletters, or blogs, each member can participate in writing. Each member can participate in seminars, or speeches. Each member can participate in one of several organizations that are part of a networking plan.

- It can be a vehicle for communication with other practice groups within the firm, thereby eliminating unnecessary communication difficulties, while sharing ideas for a common goal.

- It motivates reluctant participants by having them share in the responsibilities for the group's marketing efforts.

- It can monitor the group's plans in the firm's marketing program, to assure correct focus.

If, on the other hand, the nature of your firm doesn't lend itself to practice groups, you might consider designating a partner as the marketing partner, with the responsibility to oversee the program, coordinate the efforts of marketing professionals with the partnership, and act as a monitor and motivator to oversee participation in the program by individuals in the firm.

Client Retention

In the firm with a strong marketing culture, getting the client is only half the battle. The other half is keeping the client. It's done with more than just doing good work. In fact, most clients, surveys tell us, don't really know how good or how bad your work is. Why should they? It's not the business they're in. They have to trust the professional.

Independent studies also show that a large percentage of professional firm clients are dissatisfied with the levels of service from their accountants and lawyers. Clients are given no foundation for understanding what's being done for them, nor are reasonable expectations defined. What basis do clients have, then, for being satisfied?

The reality is that this new world is competitive in ways that it's never been before. Ask your clients how many times they've been approached by your competitors, and pursued aggressively. And then ask yourself if you can continue to be sanguine about keeping your clients happy, on a day-by-day basis.

There are, of course, some things that are clearly necessary in client retention. Getting the right client in the first place is important. Doing good work, obviously. Being responsive, obviously. Being timely in delivering promised reports and material. Being polite to clients.

But these are things that are inherent in the meaning of *professional*. It's what the client is paying for. You get no credit for doing them, but you lose clients for not doing them.

Sophisticated marketers, as well as the firm's professionals, have a strong handle on who the client company is, what the company does, what its needs are, and how to address those needs in marketing approaches. Which means that if you don't have that same knowledge, and the kind of relationship that means total involvement in the client's concerns, then you're in imminent danger of losing the client. Staying in touch with clients is not – and cannot be – a casual matter. Today's business is too dynamic, and things change constantly. At the same time, your competitors aren't resting from pursuing your clients, so you may not rest.

Client retention, then, requires more than the obvious factors of doing good work and delivering it on time. And in fact, in a dynamic business world, it's often more than a personal relationship. It's at least . . .

- **Being immersed in a client's business and industry.** Knowing enough about a client's business to anticipate problems in your professional area, and seeking new ways in which other of your services can help the client is invaluable.

- **Visible quality control systems.** You may have your internal quality control systems, but if the client doesn't know that, then the client has no reason to believe they exist. More importantly, the quality control systems should relate to the client's business, not yours. This is increasingly pertinent, following the accounting and corporate scandals of the first years of the last and current centuries, and in many respects, is mandated by such laws as *Sarbanes-Oxley*. Transparency is important.

- **Frequent contact points,** beyond the engagement. You do, of course, what you've been hired to do. But you help both the client and yourself when you send a brochure on a subject of mutual interest. Or a copy of a clipping in which you've been quoted on a subject the client might care about. Or a simple newsletter, either your own or one of the excellent packaged ones, covering information of interest or concern to the client. The social media – the blog, Twitter, LinkedIn – are particularly useful for this. The client should know you exist between contacts, between matters, between consultations.

- **Maintaining personal relationships.** Not just drinking and dining to keep the client happy, but establishing and reinforcing a sense of mutual understanding and trust. The degree to which the client calls on you for business advice is as much a matter of personal trust as it is professional trust.

The *client-driven* rather than the *practice-driven* firm is the only safe way to compete in today's market. The price of ignoring this concept? A major professional firm took a highly conservative position on a matter pertaining to a client's matter. The problem was not the position, but that the position was taken for the firm's protection, and not the client's – and the client became aware of this. There went the client.

Keeping in touch with your client is crucial because needs change. Your services change. By constantly reviewing the client's needs, you not only assure that you're giving the client the best service, and that you're maximizing the relationship, but you're also telling the client that you're concerned. And the best part is that you can identify new client concerns that require your services.

Regular client surveys also help, particularly if they are professionally done. New York's former Mayor Koch used to walk the streets of the city, asking people, "How'm I doing?" He didn't always like what he heard, but he always knew. Anybody who doesn't take active steps to keep aware of client attitudes toward the firm is somebody who likes unpleasant surprises. Thoughtful surveys are helpful. Frequent personal conversations between the client and the managing partner are even better.

Successful professionals are those who've learned the difference between *client relations* and *client service*. Both are important, but one is not the substitute for the other. In client retention, you have to have both.

It's the peculiar nature of professional services that quality plays little or no role in getting new business, except perhaps in terms of reputation. It plays a crucial role in client retention, on the other hand, if you define quality as giving the client what the client needs, wants, and expects. Most frequently, in order to know what the client needs, wants, and expects, you have to be immersed in the relationship. And you have to ask. Here, quality is not an abstraction or a hollow boast – it's a reality.

Those who are most successful at client retention are those who actively work at it. They have programs and checklists. Even small firms that are aware of the need for it have programs that focus on paying attention. They listen. They contact. They understand the economics, and know what kind of return they're getting on their investment in it.

And they know, at first hand, why it's true that keeping a client is still cheaper than getting a new one.

Living with the Marketing Culture

Some quarter of a century since the *Bates* decision breathed life into professional services marketing, the professions have gone from an arcane, firm-centered, elitist culture to the beginnings of an understanding that at the core of every successful practice is the client. We've gone from groping to sophistication in marketing, which was as new to the professions in those early days as were the first live pictures from Mars.

We've learned a lot about marketing the modern professional firm. But we've learned nothing with greater certainty than that the firm with the best marketing culture is the firm most likely to thrive in the coming decades.

That's what Professional Services Marketing 3.0 is about.

{Chapter 5}

The Risk In Not Understanding Risk

How To Understand, Manage And Avoid Reckless Risk

Risk. It's amazing that so simple a four-letter word can be so complicated. There are risks with dire consequences and risks with negligible consequences. There is risk in every human enterprise; in every trade or endeavor. We take risks, in varying degrees (and sometimes unwittingly) every day or our lives. There is even risk inherent in getting out of bed in the morning. But what – on any level – does risk really mean? Can risk be tamed?

The great Oxford Unabridged Dictionary virtually dismisses risk with a simple definition – *To hazard; to endanger; to expose to the chance of injury or loss.*

But to better understand and manage any kind of risk requires a more precise understanding of it – in fact, a better definition is needed. The value of consciously understanding the nature of risk, particularly the risk of dire consequences, is that understanding delivers the greater promise of the wiser choice.

Risk, I believe, is *pursuing a course of action the outcome of which depends for success on factors over which we have no control.*

Degrees of Risk

Obviously there are different degrees of risk, depending upon how great the opportunity to profit if you succeed, how dangerous if the risk you take portends the possibility of failure, how much is at stake if you fail. One classic misconception of risk suggests that the greater the risk, the greater the return. Not universally so. (For example, sometimes risk is necessary to minimize loss.) Sometimes, the kinds and degrees of risk overlap. And sometimes, the greatest risk of all is doing nothing, which is as much a decision as doing something. Choosing to not act is merely the obverse side of doing something, and should be considered in the same way as you would a risk in taking an action.

Is that all there is to it? Of course not. It's much more complicated than that, and the meaning is colored by context. When you buy a lottery ticket, you're risking only a couple of bucks on the slender chance that you'll make thousands of dollars. Not a risk worthy of the name (unless you're playing with your rent money). When you risk a career – or maybe an entire firm – on the chance that an innovative tax shelter program is legal, or that a litigation strategy will keep your client out of jail, that's a significant risk. When you gamble that you won't get caught embezzling from your firm, or that your imaginative tax return won't be audited, you risk jail or a fine.

When you falsify a tax return, you cannot generally control the possibility of being caught by an audit. Assuming an honest game, we can't control a horse race or a ski jump or even a card game. When you write an article or a brochure, you can't control how it will be received by its intended audience. (writers, especially the best, live with this constantly.) When you invest, you risk your knowledge and intuition against that of the volatile securities market. When you advise a client in any matter of law or accounting, there is risk inherent in the accuracy of your advice. Yes, skill and experience can often mitigate the degree of control we might have over the outcome. With skill, judgment, and experience you can eliminate some – but not all – of the factors that are beyond your control.

In marketing, there is risk that a marketing program will in some way backfire. There is certainly risk that a seminar will not be attended, that an article won't be published, that an ad campaign won't impress the marketplace. And the more extensive – and expensive – the program, the greater the risk.

Random and Statistical Risk

These and more risks are different in context and magnitude. A good mathematician can often statistically quantify the boundaries of risk, such as telling you that one in every hundred people will slip in the bathtub and break a bone, but that depersonalizes it and tells you nothing to help you avoid it. And that's only half way to understanding it. There is a caution, though, in using statistics alone to assess risk. A statistical – or actuarial – calculation that says one in every two hundred and fifty tax returns will be audited gives you a definition of possibility. But a random risk that says, for example, one in every thousand houses in America will be burglarized gives you no such safety, unless you can define why such houses are burglarized. Statistics are not particularly useful in random risk, simply because they are random, but the risk itself – and not the statistics – affords you the opportunity to take precautionary measures, simply because you know it could happen. There is, too the difference between possibility and probability.

When a random risk is combined with a decision not to take an action in a situation (or even a potential situation), there is fuel for disaster. One example is seen in the Virginia Tech tragedy, in which a deranged student went berserk and killed a number of students and professors. It would appear that by assuming that, statistically, there was little likelihood that such an act could happen on their campus, they were not prepared to cope with the aftermath. The school was not prepared to warn students about the shooter on campus, nor to respond appropriately after the event. They could have assessed the possibility – if not the probability – that a crazed gunmen might kill students. Here, too, mathematicians might still have assumed that it was likely to happen somewhere, which might have warranted simple preparation. There was no crisis plan in place, no designated hierarchy of either practices nor authorities – and so every decision had to be synthesized in a vacuum and on the spot. This, despite the vast array of articles about crisis management that abound in every industry and management course. The potential danger is greater in doing nothing than in making a choice among potential actions. Apparently, the school administration saw the risk from an actuarial – or statistical – point of view (calculating the number of such happenings and assuming that a serial shooter was unlikely to come to their school), when in fact the risk was a random event, which means that there is no statistical system that would serve to warn them other than to say it could happen. They took the risk that a mentally unstable individual would not act out on their campus, and so had no plan in place. The result was that as bad as the event itself was, it was made worse for lack of preparation.

By the same token, if we assume that our clients understand, appreciate, and cherish us, and don't act to take steps to find out if they really do, we are risking that client relationship, as well as losing the opportunity to strengthen and cement our relationship.

Crisis Management

A superb and definitive article on the subject of crisis management by Richard Levick appears in *The Marcus Letter*. Another such brilliant article by consultants Don Aronson and Bruce Heintz, addressing the importance of professional client interviews that go deeply into client attitudes, also appears in *The Marcus Letter*. I've written about it in several of in several of my books. Nor am I alone in having written dozens of internal memos on the subject for the firms I've worked for or consulted with. But is nobody listening?

This failure to anticipate random risk, whether on a school campus or in a legal or accounting practice, leads me to believe that people are unwilling to face up to the fact that, despite the small probability of its happening in most schools, the possibility that it could happen somewhere was high. This, despite the fact that a great deal of preparation to deal with crisis is easily done, and not overwhelmingly expensive.

Another consideration of risk lies in a tendency to ignore or distort reality, which can lead to a vast expectations gap. Recently, a survey of accounting firms by the Bay Street Group gives increased significance to the work by Aronson and Heintz. It uncovered the startling fact of the wide disparity between how accounting firm management perceives their own performance and how their clients see their performance. A sample of findings…

- Asked why their organizations might change CPA firms, 80% of clients blamed poor client service; but only 34% of CPAs thought that was the reason for losing a client. 38% of clients said they might change because they weren't getting the CPA firm's best people, but only 9% of CPAs cited that as a possible reason.

- In marketing, 11% of clients thought they might be persuaded by a firm's website; 37% of CPAs planned to launch or increase a web site. This disparity exists in the full array of marketing activities.

In other words, there is great risk in client retention and management activities that are based upon guessing or inadequate information derived from poor surveys. For example, in the case of the risk of losing a client, you can use professional skills and assiduous attention to the client to be sure that you understand not only the client's needs, but the opportunities to improve relations inherent in understanding those industry factors that inform his business. You can make sure that you not only understand the client's needs, but that you have the skills to serve those needs. You can arm yourself with data to afford yourself the opportunity to not only avoid danger points in your relations with the client, but, as well, to see opportunities to improve that relationship. And because of the subtleties of surveying, as Aronson/Heintz wisely point out, it should be done professionally.

Decision Making in Risk Management

Too often, we simply take risk for granted and go headlong into danger and chaos. It needn't be so. Even in view of the elements of risk over which we have no control, there are still measures of protection that can be taken to reduce a measure of risk in any enterprise.

Is there protection against risk? Yes – to a larger degree than we may realize. There are at least five things you can do …

- **Definition.** Define the risk itself. Understand precisely what the risk is. Too often, we either ignore risk or look at it amorphously. Sometimes, we simply take for granted that our skills and experience will be able to cope with whatever risk is involved. It's like throwing out a football and then running out to catch it. Sometimes it works, which gives license to continue to function in that mode. Until, with our eyes skyward and on the ball, we fall into a ditch. It's worth the time it takes to consider the risk of any action in which a bad choice could be serious, and to assess the variables. In defining risk, you may find, as well, that much risk is multi-faceted – the action you're considering may have several elements with different degrees of risk. Defining risk, and focusing systematically on it, frequently clarifies those factors that make risk more controllable.

- **Assess the risk in terms of the objectives.** You know what you want to achieve. Are your chosen activities the best way to achieve those objectives? Are the objectives worth the risk? What are the alternatives? Here, the decision tree approach is useful. *If we take path A, then this will happen. If we take path B then that will happen.* Which result can we better live with? When the consequences of an action are significant, this approach can mitigate risk, and allow us to make intelligent choices.

- **Eliminate the variables.** By defining the risk, you are able to define all the variables that affect the outcome, and find those areas that can be eliminated. Going to sea in foul weather for example, you can reduce a measure of the risk if you are sure that you have the skills in seamanship, and the safety equipment to diminish the danger, as well as the navigation and communication equipment to aid in quick rescue in case of mishap. In considering a legal strategy, the risk is tempered by knowledge, skill, and experience, all of which must be considered in any legal risk. And this is true, as well, in the world of accounting.

- **Decide.** By taking each of the three previous actions, you have a better chance of understanding the nature of the risk of your enterprise, deciding whether you have the intellectual tools and experience to see you safely through the risk, and whether the prize is worth the risk.

- **Anticipate and plan.** A crisis management plan – a *what if...* plan – is simple and inexpensive. Disaster is random, but the potential is always there. As Aronson, Heintz, and Levick point out, the risk of poor client service and losing a client exists in every practice. But most risk can be mitigated by professional client interviews. As the Bay Street Group study informs us, there is frequently a chasm between how professionals think their clients perceive them and what the clients really think.

A crisis plan may be as simples as designating a crisis spokesperson to speak for the firm with a predetermined script, or it can be an elaborate one that anticipates *what if...* Nothing is more exciting than having the press call about a client in trouble, and having the call – and the press questions – answered by whoever in your office picks up the phone.

By following this path, you can build a crisis mechanism that includes a communications system to warn people. You can designate the hierarchy of responsibility, and be sure that responsibility for all measures of the risk are anticipated and covered. These measures are inherent in every corporate crisis plan. They should be inherent, as well, in every professional firm, as in every school and community plan.

At the heart of every crisis management plan is the recognition that crisis can happen, and that the likelihood of its happening in your business or community is not actuarial or otherwise statistical, but random, and that even a random disaster can be mitigated with simple preparation.

The danger in not meticulously defining the risk inherent in an action and considering the consequence of being wrong is to magnify the risk.

{Chapter 6}

Anything You Can Do I Can Do Better

Are Accountants Or Lawyers The Better Marketers?
Does One Size Fit All?

It's not a race, nor are there prizes for the winner. But it has been suggested that the lawyers are light years ahead of the accounting profession in marketing.

It's nonsense, of course. Is one profession indeed better at marketing than the other? Well, no. Each profession is different, and to try to make the comparison would be an apples and oranges game. But silly as the idea may be, it opens a vast and intriguing question. Are there significant differences between the professions that affect marketing? Indeed there are.

The differences, obviously, derive from the unique professional skills and services offered by each profession, by the different issues and needs of the clientele, and by the way each service is performed. Within each profession, there are differences in specialties, in firm size, in firm philosophies, and in the different target markets served by different firms in the same profession. Many of the differences are subtle, many are profound. But differences there are, and they seriously affect the thrust of a sound marketing program. Moreover, as veteran consultant Terry Lloyd, a CPA and financial analyst, points out, *"Even though the lines continue to blur between the services, there are still differences in the way CPAs and lawyers are perceived."*

Do the differences really matter? Well, yes. While the professional services marketing tools are the same for both professions, the application of each of the tools in each of the professions, is different. And certainly not in the same way in each profession, nor even for any two firms in the same profession, These differences may be subtle, but they had best be observed if marketing programs are to be successful.

As competition becomes more intense, the distinctive nature of each firm in each profession, small and incremental though they may be, should be examined. In competing, every little advantage counts.

Generalizations, such as the marketing superiority of one firm over another, not only belie reality, they mask those particulars that matter. *Marcus's Third Law* is that the broader the generalization, the greater the disparity in details. And generalities don't solve problems – particularly marketing problems. Understanding the details do address problems usefully.

Seeing the murkiness of the generalization that one profession markets better than the other, or even that the same marketing techniques worked in the same way for all professions, we asked a number of leading marketers and consultants for their views. The proposition generally struck them as ludicrous. But in a fascinating twist, triggered by a notion that seemed simple and obvious, many of those discussing the idea came up with different views of the same conclusion. Their answers provide some valuable insights. Internationally renowned consultant David Maister (*www.davidmaister.com*), says *"Personally I find the proposition a surprise - I don't find the law firms ahead in anything at all and have no idea where the hypothesis comes from. It would be an exercise in futility to try to explain a fact that was incorrect."*

While the differences in the professions rarely reside in old bromides about the differences in personalities, Kenneth Wright, the former head of marketing for Ernst & Young, notes an interesting exception. He says, "Seems to me that the Tax Lawyers/CPA's are very similar (they believe that clients should come to them for their good work) versus the Litigators/CPA Consultants (who realize that they have to go get clients and show them how good they are). The first group really doesn't want to market at all - it is beneath them - and the second group doesn't need professional marketers because they know how to market better anyway."

At the same time, Richard Levick, of Levick Strategic Communications, LLC (www.levick.com) , believes that, "There are simply too many variables, and too many anecdotes pointing in all directions, to support any conclusion about one profession being more adept at marketing or intrinsically more marketing-oriented. However, a few likely truths emerge when we compare the professions.

"No law firm can touch the Big Four's marketing and, in fact, it was fear of the Multi-Discipline Practice [in which aspects of the law are practiced by accounting firms, and vice versa] that powered some of the best marketing we've seen from law firms in the last decade. Now that the MDPs have been sideswiped, it will be interesting to see if law firms relapse into marketing insensibility. I doubt any kind of study can determine that, but it's something to bear in mind when we observe marketing among the AmLaw 200.

On the other hand, says Levick, *"That said, the state of marketing among midsize and small accounting firms is dismal compared to law firms. That has a lot to do with their getting trapped in their own numbers games. Unlike the Big Four, their services are not so diversified or sexy. The nature of their own businesses discourages them from thinking they even have a right to be creative about marketing. Also, to be frank, their margins are usually too low to encourage investment in business development. Lawyers don't have that problem as much, so they're less disinclined to at least think about marketing venues where they can stick their money."*

Looking at the question from a different point of view, the international consultant Patrick McKenna, said, *"If you're trying to determine which of the two professions (lawyers or accountants) are the more advanced in their marketing prowess, I'm sorry but I think the very question is ludicrous. Be it accountant, consultants, architects or lawyers, it really doesn't matter. My experience confirms for me that when you think of marketing prowess you can divide any of the individuals or firms, in any of those professions (not by profession but by mindset) … into three categories: hawks, doves and ostriches."*

Silvia Coulter, head of the Legal Sales And Service Organization, and a pioneer in selling legal services, agrees with McKenna. *"That having been said, if you seek an answer on one side or the other with the assumption of Patrick's response, then I will say accountants, in general, are more in touch with reality – because of the numbers. Therefore, whether they choose sexier marketing approaches than lawyers, may not matter. It's who knows the client best and who can best retain and grow client share. Lawyers have all the answers in front of them and yet still after all this time, spend countless dollars on marketing people who know little about marketing, ignore those clients who make up 80% of their firms' revenues only to chase new business which we all know is far costlier to acquire.*

"Having the ability to spend significant dollars on advertising, sponsorships, training, etc., does not make a savvy marketer. Visiting your clients a few times a year (which costs quite little in comparison) seems to warrant hours of meetings with one another in a law firm to discuss whether or not they should visit clients, ridiculous discussions about what to talk about with clients, arguments (in many, many firms) about compensation and who's client it is, etc. etc."

Larry Smith, Director of Strategy of Levick Strategic Communications, adds, *"I have always affirmed that the core of all marketing is value for the client. If that is the case, then it shouldn't matter that an accountant's work is drab or a lawyer's work high-profile. Professionals must, in a sense, see beyond the specifics of their practices and focus on what can turn out to be absolutely riveting results for the buyer."*

Citing further differences, Terry Lloyd points out that, *"Some CPAs, the auditors, are supposed to act on behalf of the investing public and not be advocates for their clients. This is particularly true now after the latest round in the accounting scandals and the new rules under Sarbanes-Oxley. Tax CPAs on the other hand often start to resemble lawyers as advocates."*

Bruce MacEwen, an astute observer of the legal scene and publisher of the widely read blog Adam Smith, Esq. (www.adamsmithesq.com) adds, *"My primary reaction is that marketing – a client-focused exercise – has little or nothing to do with the nature of the actual work done 'inside' by CPAs and JD's. This may appear to miss the entire point of your thinking that accounting is more cut & dried and law more creative & open-ended (to which I heartily concur), but again, I think the aim of 'marketing communications' is to connect with the client/prospect in a way that establishes your (CPA firm/law firm) as offering a distinctive value vis-à-vis your competitive set. Again, this has as little to do with how your litigators draft briefs as a car ad has to do with the credentials of their mechanical engineers. Say I as a client, 'I want a sexy, growling, red 2-door coupe," or "I want to win this case fast, hard, and cheap,' not 'I need an Ivy League ME or JD'. To me, good professional services mar-*

keting is good professional services marketing, driven by genuine insight into the client's "need state," and speaking to that with benefits that are plausible, ownable (by your firm), and insofar as possible, unique."

But what of the particulars? How do the differences between law and accounting color the way each profession markets? How does such empirical evidence as the fact that there are infinitely more blogs by lawyers than by accountants, for example, inform the proposition? The consensus of these thought leaders in professional services, then, is that while neither profession has the obvious edge over the other, there are indeed differences in the profession that affects the nature of marketing for each.

Gale Crosley, an insightful consultant to the accounting profession and author of many thoughtful articles on accounting firm marketing, (www. crosleycompany.com) says, *"Michael O'Horo (who has consulted on law firm practice growth for the past 10 years) and I have discussed this at length, and are constantly doing comparisons, since I only do CPA firms and he only does law firms. We have discovered and debated differences, but have been unable to draw overall conclusions regarding relative practice growth sophistication between these two different ecosystems. However, if we break down practice growth into the three functional components of sales, marketing and product management, I suspect we will find differences, and maybe even significant ones. For example, the Big Four invested heavily in large opportunity methodologies and training (sales) over the past 10 years. Because they dominate the CPA firm landscape, they have set a tone at the top – significant sophistication in opportunity pursuit. At first glance there doesn't appear to be the same consistent wholesale investment in large opportunity pursuit at the top of the law profession. However, O'Horo could certainly confirm this. Within the product management discipline, CPA firms are infused with investment management niches which often incorporate a "packaged product" orientation from their roots in investment houses and insurance companies. This piece of the CPA firm ecosystem is probably way out in front of the law firms, which may not have a similar influence."*

David Urbanik, Chief Operating Officer of Halloran & Sage LLP, points to the specifics. He says, *"I have never seen this quantified, but I would suspect that the majority of the revenue earned by the typical CPA firm is derived from* what I would describe as routine, generic tasks that are an integral part of the annual business cycle, most notably the annual audit and the annual tax return. The methods and practices used to produce these two major products tend not to vary much from firm to firm and the final work product of one firm on a particular assignment on the face is probably indistinguishable from that which would be produced by a competing firm. Of course, accounting firms can and do provide other consulting services. However, I think in the mind of the average business executive, accounting services are thought of as a routine service that you purchase as part of your basic business operations.

"In contrast, I believe most law firms generate the majority of their revenue through what I would classify as more specialized services. Invariably, this leads to the ability to carve out and pursue a greater number of unique market niches than I think are available to the accounting profession. Even when legal services involve repetitive instances of the same type of service (closing a loan or defending a workers comp claim) each individual matter is in some way unique and the outcome may vary significantly depending on the skill and approach of the individual lawyer. As such, providing legal services generally requires not only the specific base knowledge of the profession but may demand a greater degree of analysis, creativity and ultimately, strategic decision making (or strategic advising) than generally associated with the accounting profession. In addition, many legal services involve a much higher degree of perceived business risk (particularly litigation). Given these facts, it is only natural for the typical business person to view lawyers as specialists hired to influence the outcome of a situation, whether it be a piece of litigation or a business transaction. As noted above, accountants are typically hired to deliver a defined product.

"Given the above distinction, I would expect the two professions to employ very different approaches to marketing. I would expect law firms to be push individual reputations, specific knowledge, and demonstrated results more heavily than accounting firms. Likewise, I would expect accounting firms to emphasize general experience, efficiency, and specific industry focus more so than law firms. Thus, many of the things law firms are doing may not even be appropriate to the accounting industry and there may not be many lessons to be learned.

"*The lesson to be learned for both professions is not to look to the other for answers. All the answers are with their prospective clients – what do they value and is what they value worth delivering (i.e. can you make a profit). Once you figure this out, the marketing challenge is to pursue those vehicles that will most likely impart information that will lead clients to conclude that you can deliver what they value as well or better than potential competitors.*"

To which David Maister adds, "*Maybe, just maybe, the explanation lies at the individual partner level. There, you could make the case that there is more entrepreneurial intuition among lawyers (even in large firms) than among accountants, but I'd bet a lot of money that if this is true, then it's driven by compensation schemes which are w-a-a-ay more individualistic in law firms than accounting firms. There are many significant differences between the practice of law and the practice of accounting (size of engagements, duty to public v. duty to client, etc.) but it would be a waste of time to list them unless we really knew what we were trying to explain.*"

And to which Larry Smith adds, "*The challenge for accountants is to start appreciating how much they are capable of being appreciated. Maybe lawyers do have a head start on that, if they're doing high-level or bet-the-farm work. Maybe accountants are weighed down in their creativity by the work they do. But it doesn't have to be if they can somehow see beyond the daily grind.*"

Based on the responses from these industry leaders, then, the foundation of the question is ludicrous, but the question itself raises valid issues that are worth exploring.

Comparing the marketing ability of one practice compared to another is irrelevant of itself, then, and leads to generalizations that serve no useful purpose. But when the question of which firm is better at marketing is addressed, it raises issues concerning the different nature of each practice. Notes Terry Lloyd, "*The Big Four are trying to create a firm brand and firm relationship with the clients. They minimize the role of the partner and other professionals. While law firms go to lengths to put impressive resumes and contact data on their web sites, it may be almost impossible to find even a list of partners on the sites of the Big Four.*"

Several of the respondents note the differences in marketing between large and small firms. Larger firms in both professions are obviously more sophisticated in marketing than are smaller firms. They have more services to offer, reputations that are, for the most part, more prestigious than smaller firms, and certainly, larger marketing budgets. While size, as Silvia Coulter points out, is no guarantee of the ability to understand marketing, the larger firms tend to hire more experienced and more versatile marketers, which sometimes – but not always – results in better understanding of marketing practices and skills.

But the real differences lie in the nature of the practices themselves. As David Urbanik points out the revenue of accounting firms tends to come from routine and generic tasks, while the law firm faces new problems – or old ones in different iterations – each day. Both are marketable skills, but the accountants skills lie predominantly in a formalized product, whereas the lawyers tend to address problems of larger dimensions, requiring innovative and distinct solutions. An audit is an audit, and because audit rules are essentially institutionalized, it's difficult to distinguished the capability of one accounting firm as better than another. Lawyers, on the other hand, see either new problems every day, or old problems colored by the nature and context of the client. The accountants must sell the ability to do the same thing meticulously well; the lawyer must sell an innovative ability to understand and apply complex law to the benefit of the client. The accountant sells the ability to confirm; the lawyer sells the ability to innovate. And as David Urbanik so cogently points out, *"The lesson to be learned for both professions is not to look to the other for answers. All the answers are with their prospective clients – what do they value and is what they value worth delivering (i.e. can you make a profit)."*

In other words, in this new environment, the client, not the profession, is at the core of the practice. (See *Client at the Core*, by Bruce W. Marcus and August Aquila, John Wiley and Sons, 2004)

It can be argued that in many aspects of accounting, consulting skills are often required, and they are certainly not static. Tax accounting requires not just a knowledge of an arcane body of tax law, but in many cases, an ability to legally apply tax practice innovatively. But here again, you are dealing with the individual practitioner, and with tax codes that are not as susceptible to interpretation as are most of the matters dealt with by lawyers.

Many law firms are better at marketing than many accounting firms, as many accounting firms are better at marketing than many law firms. The nature of the professions, remember is that individuals, or teams of individuals, practice the professions, not corporations. And while firms may be managed so that its partners are highly individualized, or may be, on the other hand, so well in tune with one another as to tend to have a better leavening of quality (what David Maister famously calls, "the one-firm firm"), individuals, not corporations, are the practitioners of the professions. It should be remembered, then, that ultimately, marketing is an art form. The skill in marketing resides not in the mechanics, nor in benchmark concepts, but in the artistry of the marketing practitioners.

Perhaps the marketing differences between the two professions lie not in the mechanics alone, but in the strategy. And the strategy works best if it's formulated with particular attention to at least two areas in two areas – the target audience and the content of the marketing campaign – but always with the focus on the needs of the clientele. The view of the differences may be discerned by looking at the services performed, and by looking at the different skills used in the practice of each profession, and the different problems each profession solves and the different opportunities sought by each profession. Herein, then, lies the incremental differences that distinguish one firm from another in a highly competitive environment.

Experience tells us, then, that three factors work best in marketing professional firms, in distinguishing the difference in professions, and in serving to distinguish (if not differentiate) one firm from another. They are...

- **Market the practice area – not the firm.** Today's consumer of accounting and legal services is more sophisticated than ever before. Clients will hire the firm – and often the firms – with the best specific practices in areas that serve their needs, which is why so many companies now have several firms to do different things, rather than one firm to do it all. Even in accounting, a company may hire one firm to do its audit, and another to do its taxes, and another to supply appropriate consulting services. Firm reputation may be a consideration, but even reputations are built on individuals.

- **Market the practitioner, not the practice.** Clients today know that they are hiring individuals or teams, not firms. Smith & Dale LLC don't do great work, but Mr. Smith and Mr. Dale do. Firms are distinguished, not by peculiar notions of brand, but by the reputations and skills of individuals.

- **Market to the clients' needs, not to the firm's view of itself.** The more *YOUs* in the marketing thrust than *WEs*, the better the marketing. Obvious? Well, apparently not, judging from most of the marketing being done. And apparently, it takes more skill and imagination to say *YOU*, than it does to say *WE*.

This, then, is what marketing professional services in the contemporary environment is about. Recognizing this reality, and focusing on it, makes the original questions about differences between professions worth exploring. Particularly so, if it leads to more innovative marketing. Then, who's better at marketing, is irrelevant.

What is relevant is which firm serves its clients and itself to better meet the needs of both. That – and that alone – is most important. It's certainly more important than which profession does it better.

{Chapter 7}

A Fixed Position In A Moving World

Positioning As A Metaphor

There is no great mystique to the marketing concept of *positioning*. While it's not as simple as some would make it seem, nor as complex as others would have you believe, it's still very real.

Like so many words used in marketing, *positioning* has come to be shorthand for some ideas that have come a long way in the pursuit of sound marketing practice. First popularized by Ries and Trout in their 1981 book, *Positioning*, the concept took a basic advertising practice and codified it in a way that made it possible for other marketers to think differently about approaches to the market.

The basic idea is simple. Or at least, simple to state.

If you think of marketing as a process to move goods and services to the consumer, there are two ways to view the process – either you sell people what they want, or you try to persuade people to want to buy what you want to sell. The second is an almost inevitably fruitless exercise in egocentric behavior. *I can make you buy anything because I'm a good salesman.* It's an uphill trudge, and yet, it seems to be the way to which most people gravitate.

Selling people what they want is obviously the better way, although it's not without its rigors. How do you know what they want? How do *they* know what they want? When nylon was invented in the 1940s, could you have asked women who had never heard of the stuff if they wanted nylon hose?

We do know that people buy what they need. They are *sold* what they're persuaded they need. And if you have to persuade people that they need something, isn't that the same as selling what you want to sell?

Not quite – if you can cast your product or service in a context that address-es the consumer's needs or concerns. DuPont solved the nylon problem by asking, "Would you be interested in hose that were as sheer or beautiful as silk hose, but wore like iron, and didn't cost any more than silk?"

And that was positioning before the word was ever used. DuPont, and other good marketers of their day, did three things...

- They defined consumer expectations

- They figured out how to meet those expectations with a product they had developed that nobody had ever heard of.

- They asked themselves, "What fact or value can we communicate to the market that would address those expectations and concerns?"

From those three points they developed the marketing campaign that sold nylons. That's positioning.

And these three points, articulated by marketing consultant Peter Horow-itz, define the clearest approach to positioning that might be used by an accounting, law, or consulting firm today – no matter what the size of the firm.

But articulating a position is hardly a total marketing plan. A number of elements must be addressed to turn a position into a marketing plan.

A caveat. There is a distinct difference, too often ignored, between a *posi-tion* and a *mission*.

A *mission* is a projection of objectives. It defines what the firm thinks its purpose is – where it would like to go in the business context... how it would like to serve its clients ... how it would like to be perceived by the community it serves. It is, essentially, a wish list and a blueprint for the company. But a mission is the company's business, not the consumer's. I say to you, "I would like you to be my friend and for you to love me." That's my mission. And you say to me, "That may be what you want, but what's that got to do with what I want? Why should I be your friend, and what have you done for me that's lovable?"

No, a mission statement is not a position.

Nor is it a niche, in which you choose a specific capability, or a specific industry, and promote your capabilities or experience in that industry to a carefully defined audience. In fact, positioning enhances both niche and target marketing.

A position says, "I understand what you want and need, and what concerns you most, and I'm going to give it to you."

In practical terms, how does it work? More caveats.

- The position must stem from the best possible understanding of the needs, aspirations, and expectations of the prospective clientele. There should be a perception of what your market most wants of a firm like yours – and that perception comes ideally from research. At least two of the top tier accounting firms have spent several million dollars each on just this kind of research. If you don't have that kind of money – or commitment – do your own survey. Ask your existing clients, your friends, their friends – anybody. But don't guess. Know.

- The position must be based on reality. You may take the position – and advertise – that you do better audits, or write better briefs. But if you can't prove it, or it just isn't so, you're ultimately going to lose more than you gain. Don't promise what you can't deliver. The acoustics of the marketplace are magnificent, and if your promise is not deliverable, you'll get caught and hung.

- The position you choose must spring from – and be driven by – your own business strategy. You've got to look at your firm… see who you are and what you want to be… consider partner aspirations… weigh skills, strengths and weaknesses. If you ignore this step, you stand in danger of not only selling a mythical firm, but of being unable to deliver what you sell.

- There are at least two ways in which a position can be determined. The first is a perception of the market needs, however that perception is arrived at. The second is to choose market opportunity. The first is a careful analysis of what the market wants and needs, and that you can supply. The second sees an opportunity that may not have existed before. Either way, the position must be reinforced in a proper marketing campaign.

- Either work with available skills, or develop new skills before the positioning program begins. It's one thing to recognize the opportunities for your firm for helping small companies because of Clinton administration proposals, and to choose a position based upon the needs of small businesses. It's another thing to have a real ability to serve those needs.

- Choose a single position point. Diverse positions are impossible to sell effectively, and each position, instead of reinforcing the others, dilutes them all. One point, one thrust. Examples cited by one expert, Paul Cole of Decision Research, are based on the observation that a customer's overall impression of a company is one-dimensional. "Pepsi, for example, is associated with youth. Volvo with safety, Burger King with flame-broiled food," he says. Most recently, an airline stressed comfort and leg room in its planes. "Only when a market has fully accepted the unique position," says Cole, "should a company attempt to build positioning extensions. Now that BMW is fully associated with full performance, it can begin to extend its positioning to luxury as well."

- Reis and Trout point out that the only company with a predefined position is the market leader – the number one company in the field. It tells the market that the market itself prefers that company. It also defines the market from which competitors must capture a share, if possible.

- Emphasis, in positioning, must always be on how the public will perceive the firm, and not on how the firm perceives itself, or would like to be perceived. The position must stem from the reality of the firm and the market, and not from an arbitrary notion of what will sell, regardless of the reality of what the firm is. Reality counts, not image. The danger in the concept of image is that it implies that symbols can be manipulated to control any image – even one that's not rooted in reality. It simply isn't true. If you don't like the perception that the public has of your reality, change your firm, not the symbols.

- When the position is determined, it must be communicated internally, even before it's communicated externally. Simply, if you're going to tell the world who you are, don't you think you should tell your own staff and colleagues first? After all, they're the ones who have to breathe life into the position, aren't they?

Given the defined position, three things must be kept in mind...

- Positions are dynamic. They should be rethought periodically, in every aspect, to be sure that they still apply. The market may change, or you may change.

- No position will work if it doesn't, in some way, differentiate your firm from others.

- The position is ultimately nothing more than a platform to project your firm's ability to meet the needs and expectations of a prospective clientele. The marketing program, in all its aspects, must be used to make that position live and viable as a marketing device.

The marketing program may be as elaborate or as simple as your budget and marketing objectives will allow, but if the position you select is to be effective, the program must spring from that platform.

In professional services marketing, the tools of marketing are used to project that platform – that singular reason for people to want to do business with you – in an integrated and concerted effort. Advertising, even when millions are spent on it, and even if the ads perfectly reflect and project the position, won't produce a single client if there isn't a well-rounded support program that includes some projection of specific capability.

And no positioning program, nor any marketing program, will work if it doesn't lead directly to the opportunity for a lawyer, an accountant, or a consultant to make a personal presentation. Which brings it all down to effective sales training.

The profound difference between product and professional services marketing poses some interesting obstacles. Bufferin can project, as its position, that it gives the relief of aspirin without irritating the stomach, because it knows that there's a vast audience of people who are concerned about the stomach problems that might be caused by aspirin.

But without making unbelievable or unsustainable promises (we do better audits/we do better briefs), how does a professional service devise a viable position?

Based on the foregoing principles, there are always specific concerns that prospective clients of professional services have. The small business owner may feel that he knows how to manage his or her business, but may be concerned about cash management, or financial statements that will help at the bank, or about tax returns that not only save money but are sustainable under audit. People are concerned that they are too small to get proper attention from a firm your size, or that they'll get the right individual in your firm for their problems, or that you even have the breadth of experience or technical skills in your firm to give them the best possible help. Every business person is concerned that you don't understand his or her business, or that you're more concerned with your business than with theirs. Addressing concerns such as these are valid and useful positions.

A position, as with any aspect of marketing, or reputation in marketing, is only as good as the way in which it's used. If it isn't constantly reinforced, it's useless. It's like a hoop. As long as you keep beating it with a stick, it keeps rolling. When you stop, the hoop falls over, and the distance it's gone is lost.

Can you market without a position? Of course. But it's like cutting a thick steak with a dull fork. It may work eventually, but it isn't worth the effort.

{Chapter 8}

Let's Lose The Word *Image*

It's A Hollow View

Some years ago, in a remarkably successful marketing move, a graphic designer specializing in logos, letterheads, and the like came up with the concept of the corporate image. A brilliant concept, but more mirage than image.

Now one of the most successful operations in the marketing business, this company has managed to persuade its clients that corporate image is the key to corporate success. *Image*, it seems, is the magic elixir. At many thousands of dollars a dose.

In fact, the word *image* itself has taken on a life of its own – a tribute to the triumph of virtual reality. But maybe it's time, now, to lose the word. The image of image is long since tarnished, and well beyond burnishing.

Words have a remarkable ability to conjure up visions beyond their literal definitions. Some words do marvelous things to the mind. *Chimera. Poignant. Vistas* – landscapes – spring forth at the mention of words such as these. But the word image, as it's used today, projects an infernal and involuted picture of things manipulated, unreal and untrue.

Image was first popularized, some years ago, by the *Father of Modern Public Relations,* the late, estimable Edward L. Bernays, and was meant to portray the pervasive perception of a company or a person. The image of the telephone company as a vast corporate universe that encompasses us all, and touches every one of us inevitably, yet maternally (Ma Bell). The image of IBM as cool, efficient, firmly aggressive, and ubiquitous in the workplace. The image of Nixon the devil and of Kennedy the saint.

What a marvelously convenient word. A company doesn't have a reputation anymore, it has an image. The perception of a company by the people who know it, do business with it, know about it, is an *image*. As if vast, complex organizations that touch the lives of many people are so devoid of facets or subtleties that they can be encapsulated by one simplistic perception. As if all of the bad or inconsequential can be submerged beneath the good and useful to make more people want to do more business with the company.

How wonderful to ponder the notion that one need not do good work, or make good products, or provide good service – one need only manipulate symbols to project a favorable image. By communicating selectively, the image purveyors seem to be saying, the public may be made to perceive the company as a personality, beyond the evaluation in the marketplace of the quality of the company's goods and services.

And anybody who believes that would believe that pornography is love.

Many years ago, at the beginning of the era when people mindlessly seized upon the term as a kind of shorthand for perception and reputation, Eastern Airlines spent a considerable sum to brighten its corporate image. A new logo was designed, with a distinctive color. It was corporate image based on instant recognition. But the clearly identifiable *image* readily focused on rude personnel, dreadful service and dreary food, planes that were always late, and constant overbooking. The symbols projected one thing. The realities shouted another. And beyond the lingering memory of its logo, where is Eastern Airlines today?

Consider, too, the image of Arthur Andersen as a classic accounting firm, with a reputation for integrity, probity, and independence. And where are they today?

The truth is that, in this context, there is no such thing as image. There is *reputation*, which can sometimes be manufactured. But reputation is fragile. It can be destroyed and blown away by the simplest element of unfavorable performance. The reputation of a company sustains only when it's built on facts, and then it isn't fragile. The pervasive perception of a company is built on performance, and sustains only when the performance is consistent. Nor is there ever, for a company, a single perception. The dynamics of business are too rapid and multifarious for that. Is the perception of a company the same to the shareholder when the dividends are increased as it is to the customer who feels that he's been given poor quality for high prices?

There is *perception*, which can be manipulated briefly. Barnum tried it with a sign in his menagerie that read, "This Way To The Egress." When his customers found themselves outside the exit door, they took it in ill humor.

The inherent danger in the word *image* is that so long as we believe that there really is such a concept, and we work toward enhancing it, we absolve ourselves of the need to nurture reputation and perception by improving reality. In fact, the acoustics of the marketplace are too good, and the truth is inevitably heard – loud and clear. Better to labor to improve the truth than to polish the image.

And so the world would be better off if we were to lose the word *image*. The perception of it is too crass, its reputation too shoddy. It keeps us from better and more useful things.

[Section Two]

Following are articles from *The Marcus Letter, The Marcus Report,*
and elsewhere that I've written over the years.
Some are from the late 1970s and the 1980s – some are more recent.
You will find, of course, some repetition, because some ideas in the
context of one article are relevant in another, written at a later date.

We've chosen these articles as representative of observations
made over the years since *Bates*. They cover the state of the art of
professional services marketing during the period I call

Professional Services Marketing 2.0.
They are as valid today as they have been since *Bates*.
They are precursors to Professional Service Marketing 3.0,
and will likely continue to be through the art of
marketing professional services for many years to come.

{Chapter 9}

The following article appeared in the September 1980 issue of The Virginia Accountant. It is probably the first – or at least one of the first – articles on post-Bates professional services marketing. It is as viable today as it was then.

Marketing An Accounting Firm
By Bruce W. Marcus
Director of External Communications
Arthur Young & Company

When, a few years ago, the codes of ethics were changed to allow straightforward marketing by professionals, there came into play a new configuration of circumstances and activities that will reverberate throughout the accounting profession for years to come.

For generations, concepts of probity have pervaded public accounting. Accountants were to be not merely independent, but well beyond the fray of public quarrel or exposure. The sword of the CPA has always been independence and, it was long felt, independence is compromised by public debate. And now comes marketing, the crux of which is visibility.

Now, after all these generations, public accountants may advertise, may compete for one another's clients, may sing their own praises, and may discuss publicly differences that had once been solely family affairs. This is how marketing has come to public accounting.

No longer do accountants compete solely on the strength of their capabilities. Today, every accounting firm – and not just the Big Eight – competes with every other accounting firm in its market area for clients present and future, for attention, for exposure. Accounting firms compete with one another – presentation for presentation, press release for press release, speech for speech, seminar for seminar, and ad for ad.

Marketing of sorts has always been inherent in building a professional practice in any profession. Lawyers go into politics and always have. Accountants have always joined organizations, given seminars, made speeches, distributed pamphlets and brochures. Competition and exposure has existed, but discreetly; performed but not discussed.

Now, it is flagrant – for good, bad or indifferent.

It poses an interesting problem. Not only is total marketing a new concept for the accounting profession, but, in searching the annals of marketing literature, we find very little to guide us. The literature of marketing is heavy with tomes on marketing *products*, but virtually nothing on marketing *services*. And unfortunately, as many a professional is beginning to discover, there is a difference in the same thing. The proven techniques of marketing a product are not strictly applicable to marketing a service. What's the difference?

In marketing a product, the product itself is the interface between the producer and the consumer. There may be a thousand people behind the production of a tube of toothpaste – but all the public sees, knows or cares about is the tube of toothpaste. In marketing a service, every individual who performs that service is the interface with its public; every individual who performs the service is, in effect, the product.

This makes it possible, in marketing a product, to centralize and focus the marketing effort. Once the product is perfected in terms of its potential market, the marketing people take over, to the exclusion of everyone else. The production people, the finance people, and the people in the warehouse are not involved with marketing. It is a separate and distinct operation.

In marketing a service, on the other hand, marketing is decentralized. Every activity performed in an accounting firm, no matter how large or small, is visible and of concern to prospective clientele.

This has its strengths and its weaknesses, as apart from product marketing. A tube of toothpaste has a consistent quality that its users can rely on. There is no consistency, however, in the human behavior inherent in performing a service. One junior accountant having a bad day can destroy the effectiveness of a vast array of advertising, public relations and other promotional efforts – an onerous burden placed on the professional. A new customer for a tube of toothpaste faces no personality conflict with the product; personal chemistry between an accountant and a prospective client can readily negate a great reputation.

On the other hand, the accounting firm that recognizes this distinction faces the opportunity to prepare and train its people appropriately to meet and deal effectively with the prospective client, and to leverage the effects of a carefully built and nurtured reputation predicated on the tools of marketing.

And here we must look at the term "marketing" in a fresh context.

Every marketing specialist has his own definition, and each can quarrel with the other's choice of words. Here again it's too easy to fall back on the structures of product marketing for a definition – "to move the product to the consumer." But if, in marketing a service, those who perform the service are the product how, then, can this definition apply?

Perhaps the more appropriate definition of marketing, in this context, would be "to define and project the service, in terms of its users, in ways that make more prospective users want to do more business with you."

How can this be accomplished within the context of the accounting profession? The answer may lie in another and more functional definition of marketing. Marketing may be perceived as:

1. Defining the market.

2. Defining the product – the service – to meet the needs of the market.

3. Defining the tools of marketing to be used to reach the market.

4. Managing the tools of marketing.

In terms of marketing accounting services, let's look briefly at how each of these elements apply.

Defining the Market

There are two points of view to defining the market for a professional service. On the one hand, a market can be defined in terms of a prospective client universe that can be served by a firm's existing personnel, capabilities, and services. On the other hand, a market can be defined in terms of the marketplace itself-its configurations and needs - within the framework of a firm's ability to adapt to those needs. The classic example might be the piano player in the cocktail lounge. Some piano players will play anything you want to hear, so long as all you want to hear is "Melancholy Baby." Others recognize the tastes and demands of the clientele, and use their piano playing skills to play the kind of music the patrons want. Clearly, it's the second piano player who works more regularly.

So it is in defining a market. The professional firm has a choice of either scouting out the clientele for the services he has to offer, or, on the other hand, determining the kind of services potential clientele need within the framework of his capability, so that he can adapt accordingly. It is the latter who is more likely to succeed in the market place.

Defining the Product

The diversity of accounting services offered by even the smallest firm is wide and flexible. If a major purpose of defining the market is to determine the needs of the market, adjusting the service to meet those needs is not only within the realm of possibility – it's an absolute necessity.

Even a small accounting firm with capable partners has the ability to amend its services to meet the needs of a larger universe of potential clientele. The need to do this becomes more acute, in view of the fact that many of the Big Eight firms are now foraging in market areas, such as small business, that had previously been considered not cost effective. What this means to the smaller firm is that it must focus in areas, and on services, that are most demanded, in which there is the least competition, and are probably not cost effective for the local office of the Big Eight firms or other of its larger competitors.

The Tools of Marketing

The tools of marketing are those disciplines that serve to project a firm's capabilities to its prospective clientele. Normally, these tools include:

- Market Research
- Advertising
- Public Relations
- Brochures and Newsletters
- Speeches and Seminars
- Direct Selling

Each of these disciplines has its place in a total marketing mix. None by itself can be considered marketing. Each supports, enhances and magnifies the others.

At the same time, it should be considered that not all of these tools, however effectively used, are useful for every professional firm. Its the mixture, the proportion with which each is used in a total mix, that count.

And each must be used realistically. Advertising may be impractical for some firms, and a most effective tool for others. Public relations, or at least the publicity aspects of public relations, may have very little to offer some firms.

In this context, it's less likely that the financial editor of a major big city newspaper will call on a small local practitioner for tax advice than on an expert from a local office of a Big Eight firm. On the other hand, with some effort and skill in dealing with the press, it's not all that unlikely.

A good article in a local accounting journal or trade publication written by a small practitioner is very much within the realm of possibility. When the article is reprinted and distributed to prospective clientele, it serves as mighty a public relations – and overall marketing – purpose for the small practitioner as it does for the Big Eight firm.

Brochures in four colors, so effectively used by large accounting firms may not be as cost effective for the smaller firm. But a simple personalized newsletter can be extremely helpful. Again, an inexpensive reprint of an article in a local accounting journal can sometimes be as effective as a brochure.

The point is that no single marketing tool is beyond the scope of any professional firm, no matter what its size, if it's used intelligently, imaginatively and as part of an overall marketing plan.

Managing the Tools

Managing a marketing effort is as important as managing any other segment of a business or practice. It must be planned, budgeted and monitored. It must have clearly defined objectives that are realistic in terms of the firm itself and its ability to perform. It must be cost effective. Merely to be able to afford a full page ad in the local newspaper is not the same as having a potential for that ad to produce results.

And the marketing program should be professionally managed. This is not to say that an outside firm is always necessary. The term "professional" is used here in the context of skill and adherence to practices that are consistent with those of the discipline. For example, a poorly written article, no matter how sound its content, will succeed in furthering no marketing aim, and will in fact be counter-productive.

In keeping with the definition that in marketing a service everyone who performs that service is, in effect, the marketing effort, perhaps the most important aspect of marketing professional services is to realize that the essence of marketing is the best performance of the service. Perhaps the greatest myth of marketing perpetuated by non-professional marketers is that marketing will sell anything. It will not. The most expensive, sophisticated marketing program will not convince a prospective client that a poor accountant is a good one. It will, however, project the capabilities of a good accountant to a larger prospective clientele.

A last major point. In marketing a service, a major consideration is frame of mind. In the highly competitive atmosphere generated by the change in the Canon of Ethics, every professional must recognize that in every relationship with a client or prospective client, in every contact, in every activity, there is an element of practice development. Marketing functions best in an atmosphere in which the concept of marketing is pervasive. Every task for a client that builds confidence in a sustained relationship must be perceived as a marketing effort. Every business discussion with a prospective client is a marketing effort.

Marketing is not merely an external discipline imposed upon a practice as it would be on a product. The marketing effort for a professional is inherent in the practice itself.

{Chapter 10}

The Secret Formula For Professional Services Marketing

It All Boils Down To Getting One Client At A Time

Here's a little secret about professional services marketing.

It always comes down to selling the individual clients – one by one.

You can talk about *strategies*, and *image*, and *niche marketing* and *branding*. You can talk about *articles*, and *brochures*, and *press* releases and *seminars*. But it always comes down to selling the individual clients – one by one.

Well…if you're going to have to do that anyway, why not start with target marketing to begin with?

One of the greatest ads of its kind, for McGraw Hill, says it all. It showed a dour, forbidding looking man, seated in a chair, glowering off the page straight at you. He is saying, *"I don't know who you are…I don't know your company…I don't know your company's product…I don't know what your company stands for…I don't know your company's customers…I don't know your company's record…I don't know your company's reputation. Now, what was it you wanted to sell me?"*

All those tools and strategies of marketing build a context to facilitate getting to the individual client prospect, and supplying a background to target marketing. In the highly competitive arena that now constitutes professional services, all of the mass marketing techniques build reputation and name recognition. They attract prospects, and define a firm as a foundation for moving those contacts into your arena. Then target marketing comes into play, enhanced by a kind of pre-selling.

This is why marketing efforts, prior to the face-to-face contact, are important.

What does target marketing mean? It means identifying and choosing your prospective client by name, and going after that prospect with a broad spectrum of techniques, supported by a mass market campaign.

Let's take it step by step.

- Define the client you want. A lot of ways to do this. Location. Size. Industry. Specialized need. Your fee range. An industry configuration that requires a specific service. Industry-related arena. Your definition, but do it in great detail.

- Identify the company or individual that fits your prospect profile – the one that best defines the kind of client you want for the kind of practice you want. Identify what it is you want to sell (and assumes that you've already determined that a market exists. Don't try to sell labor law to a community of individual entrepreneurial farmers who use machines instead of people). Then you identify the companies in your market area that you think would be great clients for you, because they fit your client profile. You find these prospects by...

  - Scouring your own lists of existing clients and prospects. There's more gold there than you think. *Why existing clients? Because the chances are that you've got clients for other of your services who don't have the slightest idea that you can do this new thing for them, and that they need it.*

  - Doing some simple secondary research. Go to a library or get online – or hire a research firm – and look up companies that you think might fit the bill. Use simple research sources, such as Dun & Bradstreet, Standard& Poor's and so forth. It only takes a hundred or so companies to start with. And how many of those companies, turned into clients, does it take to make the whole effort worthwhile?

  - Prospecting. Have a good agency do a great series of inexpensive ads that include requests for literature. If the ads are well done, and placed in the right publications, and the material you're offering is worthwhile, you will quickly assemble a terrific list of targets. Under some circumstances, telemarketing is a good prospecting tool. Or do a mailing offering a brochure.

- Hold a seminar, with material aimed at the kind of client you want. The attendees not only comprise a mailing list, but they become your first contact in a networking program.

- Devise your campaign strategy.

  - If you're playing off a specialty you have, then use that skill for a kind of mass marketing campaign. But remember, that campaign is only the backdrop for target marketing. You're still going to have to go after each company individually.

  - Identify the key people who make buying decisions in the prospective company. This is your target.

  - Deal directly with that person to establish a relationship. Write. Phone. Do a seminar and invite him or her. Set up a regimen of regular mailings – articles, reprints, brochures, newsletters, etc. Client advisories. A newsletter. Advertising in trade journals read by the prospect. Your objective, ultimately, is to build a relationship that facilitates the prospect's getting to know you and your skills and what you have to offer.

- Do it. Strategy is a wonderful word. It rolls nicely on the tongue. But to make strategy more than a buzz word, you've got to…

  - Have a plan that's realistic. No wishful thinking. Know what's doable, and who's going to do it. Don't identify and market to 500 companies if you can't cover more than 50 in one crack.

  - Be precise in your profile of your prospective client. Start with the clients you have, as a guide to what you do for them and what you can't do.

  - Be realistic about your partners' commitment. Everybody wants new clients. Everybody wants to be in the swing of marketing. Not everybody is willing to do it, or has the self-confidence and eagerness to do it. It's easy to say yes to a strategy, and then get busy with billable hours.

- Be professional in your marketing tools. Writing a direct mail letter isn't the same as writing a letter to a client. And even the newsletter you buy from a service should be looked at carefully to be sure that it's specific to your firm, your service, your market, your needs.

- Be organized. Get it down on paper. Who does what, and by when. More good plans slip away undone for lack of drive and organization and a good manager.

There's a large element of networking in targeted marketing, as there is in any professional services marketing. It can't be done from a distance, in the abstract, like product marketing. Somebody has got to get out there and meet and court the prospect, in order to make it happen.

There is one more important factor in target marketing, one that's perhaps the most important of all, especially for a growing firm.

A manufacturing company is defined by its products. A professional firm is defined by its client base, and the services the firm offers those clients.

Target marketing – choosing your clients and then going after them with whatever it takes to win them – defines your practice and defines your firm. If you are what you serve, and to whom you serve it, then you're better off hand-picking your clients than you are firing a load of buckshot, and eating whatever it is that you hit. That's why target marketing is better than mass marketing.

{Chapter 11}

Sing Me A Sonnet

Or Find Some Other Way To Inspire Me

At Microsoft, they worry about motivation. When everybody who holds any kind of a responsible job is making more money than any of them ever dreamed they would, and when they're in an industry that would pay anything to hire them away, how do you motivate people? How do you get them to stay, and to produce at the high levels demanded by Microsoft and other high tech companies?

Two ways. First, Microsoft appeals to what creative people crave most – the opportunity to do great work, and then recognition for it by seeing it used. Then they build a culture and a business to sustain that creativity. Second, they hire the right people. They hire only those people who are motivated by what they have to offer. And it works. It's one of the things that makes Microsoft a great and successful company.

Is this so difficult? Not really. Why, then, do so many companies look outside themselves and their cultures for motivation? Why the growth of the motivational consultants business?

This is a strange business, these motivational consultants and coaches. What's strangest is not what they do, it's the need of so many corporations to buy the stuff. Do people really think that the problem of motivation is so arcane and difficult that only an outside consultant, with exhortations and incantations, can do it? Or is it some protectionist scheme, in which, if it doesn't work, the responsibility is passed on to someone else?

We may not know a vast amount about the human mind, nor the emotions and how they're controlled, but some things seem obvious.

- Yes, people want to be adequately compensated, and there's little likelihood that you're going to motivate underpaid people. (You can probably overwork inspired people though, if they're not underpaid.)

- Exhortations to company loyalty don't work any more. There's too long a record by too many companies that have been disloyal to loyal workers for that route to have any credibility. Notice, the tradition of company songs hasn't done much to save the Japanese economy during difficult times.

- Productivity bonuses used to work, but in a positive labor market, where there's a shortage of people but no shortage of jobs, anything you have to offer can be topped by somebody somewhere else.

- Perks used to help, but not anymore. See previous bullet.

- Weird systems, like Oriental mind training and psycho systems, usually last all the way until the following Monday, by which time the trainers have gone on to the next suckers, and the trainees can't remember a thing they were taught.

In today's environment, then, unless you want to waste your money on training programs that enrich the trainers but don't do much for you, you're stuck with the Microsoft model.

- Build a culture that cherishes ideas, contributions, and recognition for both – that invites new ideas, and then uses them or takes the trouble to spur people onto improving their ideas.

- It should go without saying that you should start with the assumption that people want to do better, and want to feel part of a team – and then give them reason to feel that way. Trust people, and obviously, they will, trust you.

- And certainly, hire the right people. Not just the people with skills you need. That too. But people who will see what you have to offer as reward enough. A reason for performing well. Oh, and treat them well – as you would like to be treated.

- Certainly, it pays to have a sound business (which inspired employees will help you get and sustain). Nobody wants to work for a company that looks like it's going under. Particularly if it looks like management's fault.

It all beats psychobabble. And it costs less.

{Chapter 12}

I've Got A Little List

Targeted Marketing And A Total Context To Make It Work

There is much ado, these days, about niche marketing and target marketing and using mailing lists and knowledge management. How does it all come together to make sense for the smaller accounting or law firm, particularly when there's a limited marketing budget, and a limited opportunity to reach out to the marketplace?

Niche marketing is a valid concept, unfortunately inflated and distorted by suppliers of niche marketing materials. Marketing niche marketing material doesn't make the concept any less valid, although certainly a distinction should be made between the products of different suppliers. Some is clearly better and more relevant than others.

What it means, simply, is that you find a segment of the market you could or do serve, and market your experience and capabilities to that segment. The segment can be defined in several ways. It could be a geographic segment – say, a fifty mile radius of your office. It could be an industry segment, such as or health care, labor, or the construction industry. It could be a skill or specialized practice, such as litigation support, valuations for divorce, or cash management, or immigration law.

As often happens with buzz words, they tend to stray from their original meanings, and so niche marketing is now used to mean industry segment. Too bad. There are so many other useful ways to segment and address a market. And so many other ways to do it.

Niche marketing generally implies a form of mass marketing, at least in the sense that the same appeal (advertising, public relations, newsletters, direct mail, etc.) is made to a large group – a niche. Litigation support services are sold to lawyers. Estate planning is sold to wealthy individuals. But the appeal is singular. It's usually buckshot. A newsletter to all litigators in a market area, for example. You buy a list.

There's no question that this has value. But that value is limited by the fact that, in the final analysis, there are still a great many variables – and variables have a way of diluting, not enhancing, any effort. The variables in niche marketing, for example, include…

- The list. Whom the Gods would drive mad they first put in charge of mailing lists. No beast is as difficult to tame as a mailing list. Names and addresses change. There's no way to know which names are qualified buyers and which are not. There's no way to know which firms your competitors have already gotten to, and which are available to you. There's no way to know how much it will cost you to get and service any of the names on the list – and some are cash cows and some are the lean ones that eat the fat ones.

- The quality of the material you send. Ultimately, copy writing is an art form, as is writing newsletters or direct mail campaigns. You may be a better performer in your profession than your marketing material demonstrates – if indeed it gets seen at all.

- The nature of professional services marketing. Advertising and other mass marketing techniques may sell products off the shelf without involving anybody from the company, but the ultimate sale for a lawyer or accountant must still be made by a lawyer or an accountant. No mass marketing technique in professional services can ever do more than open the door to an accountant or lawyer, who must personally make the sale.

- Saturation. One need only look at the success of the leading suppliers of niche marketing material to realize that a lot of people on your block are going after the same prospective clients with the same general pitch you're planning to use.

- The ease of entry myth. Estate valuation or litigation support or intellectual property law may look like a great untapped market, but are you really qualified or staffed to do it? Or do you simply see it as a good marketing opportunity?

- The limitations of mass marketing for a professional service. Herein lies the greatest paradox of professional services marketing. You can mass market toothpaste because every tube, and its contents, is like every other tube. What you say about your toothpaste applies equally to every user, and every tube. No two professional firm clients are the same; no two professionals perform the same service in the same way. This is a vast and significant difference.

This is not to say that there aren't genuine values in niche marketing, under the right circumstances. If you have a specialty or a skill honed by experience and success with several clients, it's certainly valuable to market that skill and success to others who need that service. If you've got a lot of clients in the construction field, and have learned a lot about the industry – its practices, its rules and regulations, its charts of accounts – then marketing what you know to other construction firms is a good thing to do.

But the little secret about niche marketing is still this…

It always comes down to selling the individual clients – one by one.

Well…if you're going to have to do that anyway, why not start with target marketing to begin with?

Or better yet, why not use mass marketing techniques as a background to target marketing?

We can even give it a name. How about, *Total Context Marketing*?

What does it mean? It means identifying and choosing your prospective client by name, and going after him or her with a broad spectrum of target marketing techniques, supported by a mass market campaign.

Let's take it step by step.

- Define the client you want. A lot of ways to do this. Location. Size. Industry. Specialized need. Your fee range. An industry configuration that requires a specific service. Your definition, but do it in great detail.

- Identify the prospect that fits your prospect profile. There are several ways to do this. It begins, of course, by identifying what it is you want to sell (and assumes that you've already determined that a market exists. Don't try to sell labor law to a community of individual entrepreneurial farmers who use machines instead of people). Then you identify the companies in your market area that you think would be great clients for you, because they fit your client profile. You find these prospects by...

  - Scouring your own lists of existing clients and prospects. There's more gold there than you think. Why existing clients? Because the chances are that you've got clients for other of your services who don't have the slightest idea that you can do this new thing for them, and that they need it.

  - Doing some simple secondary research. Go to a library – or hire a research firm – and look up companies that you think might fit the bill. Use simple research sources, such as Dun & Bradstreet, Standard & Poors and so forth. Check all those online databases you've been reading about, here and elsewhere. Frankly, it only takes a hundred or so companies to start with. And how many of those companies, turned into clients, does it take to make the whole effort worthwhile?

  - Prospecting. Have a good agency do a great series of inexpensive ads that include requests for literature. If the ads are well done, and placed in the right publications, and the material you're offering is worthwhile, you will quickly assemble a terrific list of targets.

- Devise your campaign strategy.

  - If you're playing off a specialty you have (we're back to niche marketing again), then use that skill for a kind of mass marketing campaign. But remember, that campaign is only the backdrop for target marketing.

- Identify the key people who make buying decisions in the prospective company. This is your target.

- Deal directly with that person to establish a relationship. Write. Phone. Do a seminar and invite him or her. Set up a regimen of regular mailings – articles, reprints, brochures, newsletters, etc.

- Do it. Strategy is a wonderful word. It rolls nicely on the tongue. But to make strategy more than a buzz word, you've got to...

- Have a plan that's realistic. No wishful thinking. Know what's doable, and who's going to do it. Don't identify and market to 500 companies if you can't cover more than 50 in one crack.

- Be precise in your profile of your prospective client. Start with the clients you have, as a guide to what you do for them and what you can't do.

- Be realistic about your partners' commitment. Everybody wants new clients. Everybody wants to be in the swing of marketing. Not everybody is willing to do it, or has the self-confidence and eagerness to do it. It's easy to say yes to a strategy, and then get busy with billable hours.

- Be professional in your marketing tools. Writing a direct mail letter isn't the same as writing a letter to a client. And even the newsletter you buy from a service should be looked at carefully to be sure that it's specific to your firm, your service, your market, your needs.

- Be organized. Get it down on paper. Who does what, and by when. More good plans slip away undone for lack of drive and organization and a good manager.

There's a large element of networking in targeted marketing, as there is in any professional services marketing. It can't be done from a distance, in the abstract, like product marketing. Somebody has got to get out there and meet and court the prospect, in order to make it happen.

There is one more important factor in target marketing, one that's perhaps the most important of all, especially for a growing firm.

A manufacturing company is defined by its products. A professional firm is defined by its client base, and the services the firm offers those clients.

Target marketing – choosing your clients and then going after them with whatever it takes to win them – defines your practice and defines your firm. If you are what you serve, and to whom you serve it, then you're better off hand-picking your clients than you are firing a load of buckshot, and eating whatever it is that you hit. That's why target marketing is better than mass marketing.

{Chapter 13}

Managing Knowledge As A Marketing and Management Tool

What Do We Know When We Say Know?

The road to knowledge management, now well-traveled, seems to end with the science of acquiring and retrieving data. The end of that road, which was built mostly by the brilliance of computer scientists, stops where a clear understanding of the meaning of useful knowledge begins.

But with the growth of knowledge management as a discipline in many aspects of professional practice, some definitions may help forge a new direction for knowledge management that not only move the subject to a new realm of discovery, but may help find ways to make knowledge more useful as a management and marketing tool. We now seem to know a lot about gathering data, and are learning to turn data into knowledge. Knowledge must now be adapted to work for the firm, and especially for the firm's marketers.

Understanding information allows you to focus your management and marketing efforts to meet the specific needs of managing a firm, improving productivity, and designing marketing programs to meet the needs of specific markets. Well founded information can make the difference between management and marketing effectiveness, and wasteful and expensive efforts, with a lower return on the investments of time and capital.

What Is Information?

First, we know that *data* is not *information*, and information is not *knowledge. Data*, we know, are basic facts – unalloyed, with little or no value outside their own existence. To say, for example, that a tree is a tree merely defines that object. It says nothing of its structure, its purpose, its value. It tells us nothing about forests or forestry, or uses of its leaves or trunk. That a tree is a tree is *data*, not *information*.

Information is when we integrate the existence of a tree with the existence of, say, furniture. Then the facts of a tree take on a new meaning.

Knowledge is when we take the information about the tree and the furniture and use it to inform either forestry or furniture manufacture. *Knowledge management* is when we when we codify knowledge and convert it to useful information.

What Is Knowledge?

Theoretically, *knowledge* may be defined as information that is now, or may in the future be, useful in a specific context. Knowledge may also be abstract, with no immediate use or application, in which case it may serve as a foundation for an ultimate use. For example, when the laser was discovered in the AT&T labs a few decades ago, it was merely a scientific phenomenon, with no apparent practical use. The uses emerged and were developed much later.

In a business context, *knowledge* is information that can be applied for a specific and useful business purpose. For example, the demographics of a particular market are raw *data*. Analyzing that data in terms of the ability to make decisions about serving that area is *information*. Knowing how to apply that information to make those decisions is *knowledge*. Knowing how to deliver knowledge to those who can use it most effectively to meet a specific objective is *knowledge management*.

Knowledge – *cognition* – in this context, has specific properties that must be understood if the subject is to have any practical value.

- Knowledge is dynamic. Its value and quality change constantly. An illustration of dynamic information is an address in space (See Chapter 2).

- Even with the common language needed for communication, we know that this dynamic must be recognized if knowledge is to be useful. Knowledge is subject to…

  - Changing sources of input

- Changing input from the same sources

- Changes precipitated by the use of knowledge

- Changing needs for the same information or data

• Knowledge is cumulative. Nothing is often known by just one person—nor is it ever known in entirety. For example, what bits of knowledge did the Wright brothers bring together to make an airplane? Or Edison, Bell, or Morse, for their inventions?

   The same knowledge can serve different purposes. For example, an area's demographics may help the marketing department define the nature of a product. That same demographic information may help the finance department determine the cost of serving that market.

• People process information differently. Each person receives information through a screen of personal experience and prior knowledge. Give two people the same information about a company and its investment potential, for example, and one will choose to buy the stock and the other to sell it.

• Another form of knowledge is *tacit knowledge* – what we know only intuitively, but can't test pragmatically. For example, Freud's view of infant perception and psychology could only be surmised, but not tested. But if we build a system predicated on that intuition, and the system works, then we may assume that the intuition may be valid.

• Merely accessing knowledge can changes the nature and value of that knowledge. For example, accessing information about a company's stock can change the value of that information, both in the way it's perceived and in the way it's acted upon. Another example is in the botanical *Raowolfia*, whose medicinal properties were known by researchers in India and reported in Indian scientific journals, but unknown abroad. When it was discovered by drug companies in the United States, *Raowolfia* became the foundation for the pharmaceutical *Reserpine*.

- By the same token, knowledge about a market for your services becomes meaningful only when it's used to define a marketing program in terms of the needs of that market.

- The practical application of these concepts is a function of context. Knowledge of itself is one thing to a philosopher, another to a scientist, another to an artist or writer or journalist, and another to a functioning professional, a firm's management, or a firm's marketers.

Cognition for cognition's sake is a fine abstraction and academic exercise, like any pure science. Cognition to serve a process is a different science, although the two need not be mutually exclusive. But the danger of analyzing and philosophizing beyond usefulness can dilute the currency of the information.

We are concerned here with the use of knowledge in a business context – gathering, formulating and applying knowledge to the uses of managing a company or professional firm, and using knowledge competitively.

Clearly understood, a system of making knowledge useful in a business context, based on the principles described here, can be developed successfully. Is knowledge management complex? Not really, when it's developed on a step-by-step process. The important thing is that it works.

{Chapter 14}

New Dimensions In
Internal Communications

Information Management And
The Internal Communications Process

A terrific definition of chaos is when a client asks two different people in your firm the same question – and gets two different and conflicting answers.

Another form of it is when there's a crisis, and the press calls and gets somebody on the phone who hasn't been briefed – but who answers the questions anyway. There's real horror for you.

A managing partner bemoans the fact that his or her clear and well-defined vision of the firm has become so diluted by the time it gets transmitted down the line that there's cause to wonder if everybody is working for the same firm.

It's at times like these that somebody gets the idea that maybe the concept of internal communications is more than a management cliché. But how much more? Where does internal communications begin? With a firm newsletter? Or regular staff meetings? Or memos? Or the intranet?

Why do so many internal communications programs so consistently fail to communicate important information within a firm?

The answer, we find, is not in the mechanics and devices of communication, which is too often the first stop for an internal communications plan, but in the *content*. It's only when we realize the difference between content and mechanics that we can properly formulate an internal communications program that works. *Content is the gold. Mechanics are merely the vehicles.*

Technology fools us into thinking that because we have facts, we have information. We now have incredibly sophisticated ways and devices for gathering and distributing facts. But in reality, we are inundated with the flow.

Information Overload

Experience now tells us that a major cause of the failure of internal communications is trying to tell everything to everybody, randomly, and often irrelevantly. Information overload, no matter which communications devices are used, results in people not hearing information they really need. Information overload, then, means no information at all.

A basic tenet of a sound program is that not everybody has to know everything about everything. Success lies in defining who has to know what, and why.

Nor does internal communication do much when it's random and disorganized, and not focused on objectives. It does work, though, when there's a plan and a program, no matter how simple, for your own firm, no matter how large or small.

The Profound Need for Internal Communications

The consultant David Maister talks about the *one-firm firm*, in which all of the people in a firm, regardless of their specialties or positions, function together to enhance the firm and its objectives. Everybody understands those objectives, and recognize that what's good for the firm is good for them. Of the many elements that contribute to the harmoniously successful firm – *the one-firm firm* – none is more fundamental than good internal communications.

At the same time, internal communications is bi-directional. Allowing people to be heard – internal communication must work both ways – is crucial to making a firm of any size function as a solid phalanx to the marketplace.

The Cost of Poor Internal Communications

Relegating internal communications to second class status can be costly, even to the smallest firm…

- **The service promise you make to clients** can't be fulfilled, if the people who have to make the promise a reality don't understand and accept it.

- **In most firms, people go to clients,** to the offices of other firms, to other cities. With half the staff off site on any given day, an internal communications program is necessary to keep everybody informed of everything he or she must know in order to function productively.

- **In even the best run firms, turnover can be high.** That means that new people must be educated constantly, either from scratch or by updating the people who have to make the promise a reality. They must understand and accept it.

- **Motivation begins with communication.** If everybody who shows up for work every morning has a different view of why he or she is there, then there's no cohesive motivation. All the motivational speakers in the world aren't going to help.

- **If there's no clearly defined internal communication plan,** the most urgent directive, no matter how clear or simple at the outset, is garbled, distorted, and diluted as it goes down the line to the people who have to act on it.

- **Cross-selling** is doomed if the firm's professionals are uninformed about all aspects of the firm's range of skills and experience.

- **There is a great deal of information** that must be imparted to every individual in the firm. But each person has a different degree of responsibility, experience, and access to the firm's practices. Each must use the information differently. Each bit of information means something different to each individual in a firm.

- And of course, there's always *the need to fight rumors and misinformation.*

These compelling reasons dictate that internal communication not be arbitrary or random; that carefully designed programs are both necessary and cost effective.

A Strategy

What do we want people to know, think, or feel as a result of our internal communications efforts, and why? The answer to these questions are the foundation for any communications activity, internal or external. They define the dynamic of the program, its focus, and its program goals. They make possible a foundation for defining and shaping the strategy.

There are three crucial concerns...

- **What do we know as an organization?** What we know defines the information that must be imparted, and to whom. It is the information that must be categorized and evaluated. It is the substance of the communication process.

- **How can we create more value from it?** We can define which pieces of information go to which internal or external audience. What information best enhances and leverages the skill, knowledge and experience of each individual in the firm? Understanding and organizing what a firm knows creates value by understanding how that information can be used to the best interests of the firm, and how it will be used to serve the firm and its clients.

- **How can we learn faster than competitors?** We can learn faster than competitors by applying the defined and refined information to the firm and its practice. When knowledge, unfettered by extraneous information, is focused and directed to the individuals who can make the best use of it, streamlined information becomes infinitely more useful than it is with just random facts. Information management is the key.

The Process
By defining and classifying information, people will get only the information that's meaningful to them, unencumbered by irrelevancies.

- **Defining information.** What information do we have? What specific information must be imparted to each group? What information is mandatory for a firm's professionals, but not the non-professional staff? What information is optional. Some information is urgent and crucial, some important but not urgent, some interesting and useful on a particular level. Six kinds of information to consider are...

- **Professional.** Information pertaining to the profession itself, such as new regulations, rulings, laws, etc., and the firm's professional skills.

- **Proprietary.** Information that gives a firm competitive advantages, or that might be harmful in the wrong hands. Firm plans and strategies, for example.

- **Creative.** Original ideas and new uses of old ideas in practice development and management and client retention.

- **Opportunistic.** Information that can lead to improvement in the practice, or to competitive advantage.

- **Anticipatory.** Information that anticipates opportunity or crisis.

- **Competitive intelligence.** Important for understanding trends, ideas, competitive strategy.

The information needed by each group is then organized and codified. For example, all lawyers or accountants in a firm responsible for practice development should be aware of the marketing program, but only partners may need to know long term strategic plans. The entire firm has to know about changes in certain firm procedures, but only secretaries may have to know about nuances in word processing or rotating work schedules. In each practice group there are some things that every member of the group should know. There are some things that professionals in other groups should know. Social events should be accessible to everybody, and clearly defined as such, but shouldn't clog sensitive business communications lines. In anticipating a crisis, it is prudent to keep everybody in the firm aware of the crisis, but the core details and crisis management strategy need only be known to those who must deal with it. This should lead to pertinent information being more readily accessed, appreciated, and useful.

- **Acquiring information.** When people understand the kinds of information the firm is looking for, and the benefits that individuals get in return for supplying it, then the process has a greater chance of functioning well. Feedback mechanisms are crucial. Two factors are important – *be specific in defining the kind of information you expect each person to contribute, and use devices to streamline the process, such as forms that can be filled in simply.* Motivate and educate the office support staff to gather and transmit important information.

- **Spreading responsibility.** Unless you want to maintain a staff of professional internal communicators, you are going to have to establish a process that can be performed effectively by a firm's professionals and staff. Practice group leaders have the responsibility to communicate within their own groups. The managing partner, in running the practice group structure, has the responsibility for inter-group communication, and so forth.

- **Manage the operation.** Internal communications programs don't work by chance or good intentions. They must be organized and managed, with written agendas, plans, schedules, and attention to the details of defining, sorting and classifying information. Appropriate systems and mechanisms must be established. It's a task that should be in the hands of a dedicated information specialist – a marketing director, a librarian, or an information technology director. It's important to realize, though, that it is not a low level job.

Information Categories

While the substance of information varies from firm to firm, there are some general categories to consider...

- **The firm's goals** within the industry (e.g., share of market, quality leadership, shareholder value, increased productivity, and so forth).

- **The firm's business plan and strategy.** Firm policies and strategic information, much of which may be confidential. New practice areas, new territories, new opportunities. *Not everybody has to know everything, but everybody has to know something specific.*

- **Daily firm business.** Matters concerning firm day-by-day operations, such as medical plans, and secretarial scheduling, pension and health benefits, holiday schedules, expense rules, and other housekeeping information.

- **Professional information.** What each professional needs to know to enhance his or her professional skills and practice. To remain competitive, key people have to know the latest rules, regulations, laws, findings, results, and both technical and client related techniques.

- **Morale factors.** Social information, softball scores, weddings and births, the company's progress and what everybody has contributed to it, and addressing adverse rumors. Specific opportunities at every level, such as sales incentives, rewards for increased productivity.

- **Crisis control.** The mechanics of dealing with a crisis, how to handle inquiries from the press, how to handle rumors, and what to communicate to staff. A prime consideration here is the concept of *no surprises*. People who might have to deal with others outside the firm (such as the press) should be aware of crisis information and the process for dealing with it. Crisis management is a function of anticipation and planning before the crisis occurs.

- **Client information.** Information about clients that should be shared by others in the firm, such as new clients and new client matters, cross-practice needs and opportunities, etc. Who the clients and customers are, who the key people are, who does what for each client, matters pertaining to best serving the client. Some of this may be sensitive; some may be housekeeping. The housekeeping information goes to everybody administratively responsible; the sensitive information only to those who must perform for the client.

- **Firm performance.** New clients, new business from old clients, cases won, projects completed, feedback on the effectiveness of the firm's activities, etc.

- **Marketing.** Firm, practice group, and individual marketing plans and activities, techniques, opportunities, and results. Press releases, new firm literature, new ideas. A firm's marketing position is everybody's business.

- **Competitive intelligence.** What other firms are doing in every aspect that you can discover. Not as benchmarks (which can be retrogressive), but for market trends, ideas, and opportunities.

The Mechanics and Devices
The possible vehicles for internal communications are finite, although imagination may breed innovation. Each vehicle has its purpose, and each its advantages and disadvantages. None is better than others, but value depends on how each is used. In a well-devised program, communications vehicles reinforce one another (E-mail combined with hard copy memos, for example). Among the more standard vehicles are…

- **Intranets.** An intranet (an internal web site) can be a great tool for internal communication. You can get a lot of information to a lot of people in a very short time. The danger is in not categorizing information.

- **Face-to-face meetings and internal seminars.** They are the ultimate form of targeting information, because they allow interpersonal relationships to be enhanced, and offer the opportunity to ask and answer questions, using graphics and audio-visual material to explain and clarify. Unfortunately, the larger the firm the more difficult it is to rely on this method as a primary source of general information.

- **Internal newsletters.** Properly done, a great deal of general information can be conveyed. Firm newsletters that are well written are usually read, and can be a friendlier way to discuss general firm policy than are memos and booklets. Internal newsletters are increasingly being replaced by intranets. To be most effective, newsletters segmented by target audiences should be considered.

- **Electronics.** E-mail has changed internal and external communications, but with its popularity has come e-mail pollution – a glut of dubious information in which, like some electronic Parkinson's law, the message expands to fill the available space on-line. Closed circuit television, video, and teleconferencing, can be very effective when several cities are involved, and the extranet allows firms to integrate their own intranets with the client's.

- **The social media.** Increasingly used, internally as well as externally, are the social media, such as Facebook, Twitter, LinkedIn, etc. They should be used knowledgably, because they are impossible to erase, and they are widely read outside the firm.

- **Bulletins.** Distributing advance copies of an ad campaign, for example, makes people feel part of the campaign, and privy to something positive before the public sees it. Distributing copies of press releases internally informs and energizes people.

- **Policy manuals.** Sometimes policies and procedures are too complex not to put in a manual. Still, manuals are not a prime communications document – they're a reference tool. Any policy that's active should be communicated by newsletters, bulletins, and meetings.

- **Memos.** As terse and succinct as possible, to the point and focused, memos impart specific and cogent information. Memo writing may border on art (or, as Lord Chesterfield said, "Had I but the wit to be brief..."), but people can learn to write better memos, sans platitudes and clichés.

- **Practice group meetings.** The practice group concept is becoming increasingly popular in professional firms. A well-run practice group is a laboratory for certain kinds of internal communication. Practice groups, formed by a firm's professionals with the same practice areas, skills, or markets, are distinctive units within a firm that serve a number of important needs. Properly managed, and integrated within a firm, they address best practices, strategic plans, marketing to target audiences, and both external and internal communications. The members of the group share the group's purpose in common, and each member is generally aware of the information he or she needs. A monthly one-page summary of each group's activities circulated among all groups is an excellent way to keep everybody informed of what each group is doing.

- **Training programs.** A training program is its own form of communication, assuring that within the subject of the program, every participant is learning the same thing.

- **Word of mouth and rumors.** This is the form of communication that prevails when there is no other communications structure. It's ultimate effect is to breed discontent; it's result is to distort. It can destroy the best of firms.

These are the key methods of communicating internally. There are, of course, other devices. The bulletin board at the water fountain and coffee machine. Faxes. Computer to computer transmissions of data and text. With today's technology, there's no shortage of internal communications devices.

Success, remember, is not in the mechanics. It's in the policy and the planning. It's in the effective use of each vehicle. Without clear objectives, without a plan, without managing the plan to meet the objectives, internal communication becomes simply messages written in chalk on the sidewalk on a rainy day.

Conclusion

Effectively imparting information depends upon better understanding the nature of all firm information, the value of each kind of information to each segment of the firm, and the structure to categorize it. It's the information that matters, not the vehicles to convey it.

Ultimately, the basis of successful internal communication evolve into two areas - motivation and information management. It is here, not with the mechanics or communications vehicles, that the process should begin, if there is any progress to be made in successful internal communication.

{Chapter 15}

Dealing With Clients
Who Think They Know Marketing
But Don't And What They Should Know

There's a wonderful cartoon in which a guy in a business suit is looking over the shoulder of an artist at his canvas. The caption, spoken by the artist, is "I used to dabble a bit in accounting, too."

Then there's the guy who said to me, "If you're smart enough to be a lawyer, then you're smart enough to do your own advertising." To which I replied, "Yes that's true. You're also smart enough to be a nuclear physicist – but it doesn't make you one."

There's the guy who read a book about tightrope walking. He knew everything about tightrope walking – except how to do it.

The point is that while marketing may not be nuclear physics, it does have its craft, its artistry, its techniques, its experiences, and its history. And if you're not within the realm of all those things and more, you don't know much about marketing. Marketing mythology doesn't count for much.

And it's not just accountants and lawyers who fall prey to the egocentric nonsense that they can do it because, after all, they have graduate degrees. A large number of people in business feel the same way.

Every marketing professional can tell you a story about a client or employer who retained the marketer for the marketer's expertise, and then drowned him or her with useless second guessing. A favorite starts with the words, "My wife says..."

But perhaps the real problem is not the presumption of knowledge where none really exists, it's in the drive to an unwarranted expectation that leaps over a large mound of reality. Every marketer has a story about being hired by a professional who says, "We've been a small firm for 15 years, and now it's time for us to be a big firm. Help us." Followed by a large fee or salary, which, unfortunately, always makes it harder for even the wisest of us to say no.

Too bad, because what usually happens is not only acute second-guessing, but entrenched ideas steeped in marketing mythology. Your marketer says, from the depths of experience, "This is what we have to do," To which the reply is, "But we've never done it that way. Let's do it the way we always have." The tenure of the marketer in that situation is rarely longer than three months, at which point the client goes out to find another marketer, and the cycle is repeated.

The client, truth told, may think he or she wants to be big – but doesn't want to go through the rigors of *getting* big. Don't dislodge the status quo.

What, then, should clients or employers know about what they don't know – in order to really benefit from the knowledgeable, experienced, and thoughtful marketer? A lot, but let's start with…

- Marketing has specific skills that improve with experience. How to understand the client's market. How to write a program that achieves a marketing objective. How to use the tools of marketing, and how to manage those tools.

- Marketers understand what works and what doesn't. Many years ago I developed an ad campaign for a client who had some ideas of his own that he wanted to try out. OK, I said, let's run your ad, which seemed to be a good one, against my ad, which he didn't like as much as his ad. My ad out-pulled his by 50%. Why? Because he didn't understand the psychology of advertising, which is learned only after long experience. Remember Exxon's "We put a tiger in your tank"? It beat the stuffing out of everybody else in the field. Why? Because the guy who wrote it understood that what sold gas was not just the words, or even the picture. It was the feeling that the strength and power of a tiger became yours when you got behind the wheel. The guy who wrote it didn't learn how to do that in accounting or law school.

- There is no greater artistry in marketing than in direct mail. Knowing how to capture the reader in the first line of the letter. Knowing how to time a mailing. Knowing how to get the reader to think that the bright idea to buy was the reader's, not the writer's. And that's just a sample of what the professional marketer knows. "Why are we paying this guy so much for direct mail?" an accounting firm partner once asked. "I've been writing letters all my life. I can do it."

- Marketers understand that trying to tell people how to think about the firm doesn't work. That's why you can't say things like, "We put clients first," or "We do high quality work." It may be what you want the reader to think about you, but they're not going to just because you ask them to. More brochures are expensive and useless garbage because they attempt to get readers to believe things that just aren't credible by simply expounding them. Professional marketers know better.

- Good marketers understand the difference between firm objectives and marketing objectives. They're not the same, although you can't have one without the other, as the song goes.

- Ultimately, marketing is an art form that uses skills, techniques and experience to achieve its ends. As we've said, if you want a good marketing program, don't hire a mechanic, hire an artist.

As a professional, you should have some inkling about how expensive it is to hire marketers whose work you don't understand or appreciate, only to have a frustrating parting of the ways. It's even worse when you have a strong feeling that marketing is something you have to do in this competitive environment, but aren't quite sure about how to hire, much less understand and live with, that peculiar breed of professional services marketers.

And now a word to clients and partners who think they know marketing. Unless you're that rare bird who's had some successful experience because you have some kind of inborn talent for marketing – and there are some of you like that – you don't know beans. And you won't know beans until they start teaching marketing in law or accounting schools, which is long overdue. Or until you've had long experience with a terrific marketer on your staff. But if you don't have a natural affinity for it, there are things you should know that will result in your competing successfully in this wildly competitive market. Or until you hire marketers who know their stuff, and can teach you what you should know.

[A caveat. There is emerging a new kind of professional – an accountant, a lawyer, or a professional firm manager who is of a new generation. This individual is part of the new trend of professionals who are not constrained by the traditions of elitism that segregated the professional from the marketer – who understands the dynamic of marketing professional services, and, as well, understands that marketing is an essential part of firm management. This new professional is part of the dynamic of the new Marketing 3.0.]

You should know, first, that the mechanics of marketing – the media relations and the writing and the direct mail and seminars and such – are not marketing. Marketing, in the final analysis, is an art form. The mechanics and tools are not the art. And as I've often said, when you're hiring a marketer, don't look for a mechanic – look for an artist.

OK, then, how do you hire an artist to do your marketing? Even before you talk to your first interviewee, or read your first resume, you need to know this…

- Understand and respect the skills of marketing. You can understand a lot, if you don't try to gum it up with trying to do what you're not trained to do.

- Don't take seriously the opinions of non-marketers about technical marketing matters. They're not likely to know. Some of the best articles, brochures, and other written marketing material wouldn't pass muster for a 7th grade grammar teacher. But know that marketing writing isn't designed for grammar teachers. It's designed to communicate ideas clearly and persuasively, with credibility and passion. Writing ain't wordsmithing, any more than fine cabinet making is just hammering and sawing. It's communication of ideas.

- At the same time, know the difference between promotional activities, such as activities that enhance name recognition and reputation, and actually getting clients to build a practice. The difference is strategy, and a range of practice development activities that get you in front of prospects. Promotional activities are important, but won't do much to get you clients if you don't follow up with practice development activities.

- Either trust your marketer's judgment, or get a marketer you do trust. No, your wife, who has a degree in English and did a fine job of raising your children, can't write your brochure. She doesn't know how. And the consensus of your partners about marketing copy is about as useful as your marketing team's consensus about an audit or a brief.

- Read resumes carefully, and know (or find out) the differences between different kinds of marketing professionals. In the early days following *Bates*, one Big Eight accounting firm hired its first marketing director from an ad agency. But the guy had been in ad *traffic*, and knew nothing about professional firm marketing, or how to write press releases that someone would publish, or a brochure. "But he worked for a major ad agency," was the excuse.

- Make sure that both you and your prospective marketing hire both understand the same things about your marketing objectives, and that both of your objectives are realistic.

- Make sure you both understand what you're willing to do – or not do – to achieve marketing success. Most marketing activities, particularly as prescribed by good marketers, might not be within your experience. But they should be within your marketer's experience. Again, either trust your marketer or get a new one.

- Understand that it's a distinctive quality of professional services marketing that it can't be done without the full participation of the professional.

- Listen to what your marketer has to say. Listen carefully. If you can't live with what's being said, either don't hire that person, or forget about marketing. You'll waste your money and the marketer's time.

- If you don't know how to hire a marketer – and if you've never worked with one before, why should you? – then learn. There are good books. There are articles. There is, of course, *The Marcus Letter* and other good marketing blogs and web sites. You can speak to marketing professionals in other firms that have successful marketing programs. There are the marketer's associations – Legal Marketing Association(LMA) for law firm marketers, Association of Accounting Marketers (AAM) for accounting marketers.

- It sometimes helps to judge a prospective marketer's experience by the questions he or she asks you in an interview. A good marketer should ask...

  - How many practice areas do you serve?

  - Is there a marketing committee? How often does it meet?

  - Which are your strongest practices? Which are your weakest?

  - To whom will I report?

  - How many partners are sympathetic to marketing and supportive of the marketing operation?

  - How strong are your cross-selling activities? (This will tell whether the partners cooperate with one another, or whether the firm is a collection of individuals who think of themselves first and the firm second.)

  - What are the industries you're strongest in, and which are your weakest?

  - Do you use client service teams? How many? Which practices? How are they organized and how are they monitored?

  - Will I be able to regularly attend practice group meetings?

  - How large is the marketing department?

  - How large is the marketing budget?

  - How will marketing success or failure be judged?

Any marketing applicant who doesn't ask these questions – or questions like these – is going to be gone in 18 months or less. Don't waste your time or the applicant's time.

At the same time, it helps to hire the best marketers if you consider...

- Whether the applicant asks the foregoing questions.

- The resume is only the tip of the iceberg. If it merely lists jobs, ask what responsibilities each job actually entailed, how they did it, and with what success.

- Get an assessment of how much they actually know about your profession. It may or may not be much, but the longer the experience the greater the knowledge.

- Successful marketing requires a great many different skills – writing for many different kinds of media, from brochures to press releases; networking; strategy; media relations; planning and running seminars; list management; and many more. Ask which skills the interviewee has, and in which he or she is the strongest. Don't ask about weaknesses and expect a straight answer.

Unless you're that rare bird who's had some successful experience because you have some kind of inborn talent for marketing – and there are some of you like that – you don't know beans. And you won't know beans until they start teaching marketing in law or accounting schools, which is long overdue. Or until you've had long experience with a terrific marketer on your staff. But if you don't have a natural affinity for it, there are things you should know that will result in your competing successfully in this wildly competitive market. Or until you hire marketers who know their stuff, and can teach you what you should know.

Thinking in terms of the foregoing, and not what you think you know about marketing but probably don't, will more likely get you an effective marketing operation – and knowledgeable marketers as well.

Why do some firms succeed and grow, empowered by great marketers and marketing programs, and others don't? Start from the beginning of this chapter and read it through again.

{Chapter 16}

All Together Now – It's *Our* Client

The Client Service Team As A Growing Phenomenon

It has long been the accepted tradition, in law and accounting firms, that what's yours is yours and what's mine is mine. In other words, "I love you Charlie. You're a great guy and a great partner. But keep your hands off my clients." And thus was the lie put to the myth of cross-selling.

But things change. For example, frank competition, once anathema to the professions, is now well woven into the fabric of professional practice. The nature of the clientele has changed, somewhat drastically. Today's client rarely uses just one law or accounting firm, rarely accepts advice unquestioningly, rarely accepts non-detailed bills (and so will go, eventually, the billable hour). The day of the naïve client is now in its twilight.

At one point in the dynamic motion of client service, it began to dawn on lawyers and accountants that clients, particularly large ones, are best served by more than just a partner with a staff of lesser lights. For one thing, in today's economic and regulatory environment, the level of expertise, and the variety of skills demanded by clients, is greater than that available from the traditional partner and second team. For another, the needs of a larger client, particularly in law firms, may transcend the skills of just one practice group. The real problem here is that this kind of client need breeds invitation to second and third additional specialized firms, which can make serious inroads into the primary firm's client relationship.

An earlier solution to this configuration of client needs and the attempts to meet those needs has been the practice group, a marvelous invention, superbly chronicled and shaped by Patrick McKenna and David Maister in their book, *First Among Equals, How To Manage A Group Of Profession-als.* What was remarkable about that book was that it was the first to set forth rules for managing lawyers and accountants who, among other things, might otherwise tend to compete with one another within the same firm. Without understanding that concept, it might well be extremely difficult to get lawyers and accountants, each of whom has his or her own song, to sing one song in four part harmony. In other words, getting lawyers and accountants, proud professionals and individualists all, to sing as one team. Thus, the client service team.

In a sense, groups of professionals functioning as teams are not really new. And certainly, the value of teamwork in all aspects of industry and commerce, if more praised than practiced, is no secret. Rarely, in recent years, has any firm with more than a few partners, pitched a prospective client solo. While the implication is that the client will be served by the larger firm, and that there actually is a larger firm, that presentation of bodies is more often than not just a show. New business teams, however, are not client service teams. True client service teams go much farther than that, although the body of experience and expertise in developing and managing these teams, while growing, is still scarce and cherished. Moreover, building a genuine client service team that combines the skills and talent of the individual team members into a powerful client serving phalanx is no casual or simple matter.

Once a novelty, a growing number of firms have discovered the benefits of using the client service team as an approach to dealing with larger clients, for both better service and better client relations. Professional firms tend to be spare in accepting new ideas and concepts. But now, the time of the client service team has come. And as firms see other firms use them successfully, and begin to understand the value of the concept, they may seem willing to try it. They begin to understand that with client service teams, clients benefit from the combined brainpower of the well-chosen and well-run team, the firm benefits by both demonstrating the depth of its skills and by the extensive access to the client's business, and the firm has a competitive advantage in its extended presence and greater ability to serve clients. With this access, the firm has greater rapport with the client, and more intensive access to the client's thinking and response to the firm's efforts.

While some firms have explored the idea of client service groups, and leading thinkers like Patrick McKenna have been training firms in the concept for several years, few firms have developed the art and science of the team as successfully as the Washington-based law firm, Akin Gump Strauss Hauer and Feld. Under the aegis of its brilliant and energetic client service advisor, Iris J. Jones, and with the full support of its chairman, Bruce McLean, Akin Gump has so finely tuned the team concept that as of this writing, it now serves clients with more than 65 highly skilled, powerfully effective teams. A lawyer with a strong practice background, Jones was brought in to Akin Gump in 2003 to establish the team concept. What she has done most brilliantly is inculcate the concept within the highest echelons of Akin Gump's management, and then develop a system to build the teams effectively on almost a production line basis, without losing the individual identity and value of each team (or its members) in working with the distinctive needs and opportunities of each individual client. A truly remarkable feat.

She is repeating the feat now at Chadbourne & Parke, where she heads the firm's marketing operation. As a consultant, she is now CEO of Alchemy Business Strategies.

That Jones is so successful is no surprise, considering her background. With a J.D. from The Thurgood Marshall School of Law, Texas Southern University, she has served as an assistant attorney general of Texas, and as director of the city of Austin's law department, supervising 50 in-house attorneys. She has been in private practice in two prominent Austin law firms, and has served as an instructor and trainer in many aspects of legal practice. To this background, which affords her a full understanding of the law firm and the client relationship intricacies, she brings an extraordinary organizational skill. If, as has often been said, managing lawyers is like herding cats, she has mastered the art of herding cats.

The team concept begins, she says, with helping a firm's senior managers understand the concept and values of a comprehensive client satisfaction program. This goes beyond simply supplying legal service on demand. It requires a willingness to understand and penetrate the client's business and business and legal needs. It requires that present and future team members understand the need to cooperate on a very high level without giving up individual status or initiative. With management backing, some 70% of the firm's partners attended courses run by the William J. Flannery training firm of Austin, Texas, which emphasizes working in teams. The courses are not just motivational cheer leading, but rather intensive training in the skills of cooperation and collaboration. Presentations about the client service teams were presented at partner retreats, which further built enthusiasm for the program.

A second necessary element is a good client relationship management or knowledge management system that tracks information about clients, appropriate aspects of law, firm activity in behalf of the client, and measures firm performance. It serves, as well, to track team activities and performance.

A third necessary element is a good strategic plan for the firm, which will ultimately shape the strategic plan for each team in serving the team's client. The strategic plan is inherent in the success of a client service team structure. "The traditional approach to strategic planning involved long and protracted processes, requiring a series of meeting with individuals possessing varied self-interests, personal agendas, and a lack of focus or direction," says Jones. The results of such planning approaches, she says, were plans that participants didn't support, nor from which they got clear direction. The result was that plans supposed to cover the following three to five years became obsolete well before that.

The traditional idea that high quality and high value services are enough to be successful in a competitive global market is a myth, Jones suggests. A sound and realistic strategic plan, she says, is a foundation for superior performance, she says, and high quality alone is not enough. "Exceptional performance and client service of the highest quality are essential elements in expanding relationships with current clients and are the critical ingredients in capturing new and loyal business relationships," she points out, "But functions best only within the context of a strategic plan." And it is this exceptional performance that the team is capable of consistently delivering.

The contemporary strategic plan, she says is a function of defining the market, defining the firm in terms of its ability to serve the market, and developing a strategy to help the firm meet the needs of the market. But it's the clientele, not the firm, that's primary in a sound strategic plan.

It should be noted here that the client service team is more than a group of partners gathered together to descend on clients. The team is a complex organism, trained to function as a team, in the firm's service to the client. It functions with a strategic plan that's predicated on the firm's own strategic plan. Its members are chosen specifically by the needs and opportunities of the team's client, are well-trained in the process, well-indoctrinated in the client and the client's business, and assiduously monitored. Thus, the need for intensive commitment to the process. And the need, as well, for a culture of collaboration. Collaboration and teamwork, she notes, are not learned in law school. And while every firm may have its stars, the well run team doesn't submerge the star's talent, but rather, magnifies it .

"The first step in the process of collaboration," says Jones, "is that the firm or business entity must define its place in the market for the services it provides. The core practices or products must be must be defined and designated first and foremost in order to clarify for the internal team the firm's priority, and the client's expectation from a team of talented professionals."

Forming a team begins with a basic understanding of the client's business and needs. This is a foundation for selecting the disciplines from which the team will be assembled. Members of the team may well include lawyers from several offices, which not only assures the most appropriate team for the client, but serves the firm's practice offices by offering the firm's full range of services regardless of the offices or the client's location. "The most successful team," says Jones, "select the members who have the talent to match the needs and challenges of the client."

Many law firms, Jones notes, are not yet willing to address attorney performance issues that arise from time to time while serving the needs of a client. "It's sometimes awkward and often difficult to confront relationship managers or the service providers of a client when the performance, communication or service delivery is not consistent with client expectations," she says. "However, it's an essential step to identify and address the failure of a team or an individual team member in order to quickly respond and remedy the problem."

Given an understanding of the client's needs and problems, the team is then formed by selecting the several lawyers best able to meet those needs. A client service team member is selected based on what the member's skill and experience can bring to the team to add value to the benefit of the client first and foremost. As new opportunities for client service are identified, the team may be expanded with appropriate lawyers. A client service team leader is appointed for each team by senior management and is responsible for...

- Serving as the relationship manager who is responsible for knowing the client needs and desires
- Communicating vision and direction to the team
- Coaching team members
- Scheduling team meetings and reviewing team's progress
- Evaluating team members and providing feedback on performance and service
- Rewarding and recognizing team member contributions and successes
- Coordinating firm resources, lawyers and support staff
- Identifying best talent to work on specific client projects
- Building commitment, confidence and consensus
- Taking leadership role in action planning

In addition to bringing their skills and experience to the team, client service team members are responsible for:

- Learning and understanding the clients business
- Understanding the firm's capabilities
- Identifying problems and opportunities
- Coordinating and sharing client information
- Developing and sharing ideas for new services

- Attending and fully participating in team meetings

- Taking ownership of the action plan

In serving the client's needs, the team establishes a successful business partnership with the client. Inevitably, this results in adding value and benefits to the client. This coordinated approach improves communications, allows for consistent advice, and helps build a long-term relationship that serves to achieve the client's global business objectives. The teams objectives are met through the team's strategic plan, in which each team member has a defined role and responsibility.

By frequently discussing the client's expectations, the team is better able to understand the scope of the work, including staffing expectations, budgetary forecasts, and the necessary level and frequency of communications of information regarding the project.

A significant part of the team process is to keep abreast of the client's satisfaction with the firm's service. This is essential to client retention, as well as to keeping the team's strategic plan on course. The questions to be asked, either in ongoing discussions or by formal survey, are...

- How are we doing in providing legal or other services?

- Are we communicating with you according to your preference?

- Are we keeping you well informed?

- Are there any concerns about the team leader or the team members serving you?

- Now that we have met your expectations, what can we do to exceed them?

Accountability, an integral factor in the team concept, is important for monitoring and measuring the successful accomplishments of the team, as well as for tracking the responsibility of individuals to the team. Team leader accountability reports, team member evaluations of the leader, and team leader evaluations of team members are among the tools the firm uses to monitor team performance and client satisfaction.

Ultimately, the goal of the client service team process is to apply a systematic approach to all significant clients so that the opportunities to serve their needs are maximized. The success of the client service team initiative is its ability to build high-quality, enduring relationships through teamwork and a commitment to using the firm's best resources. "Dedication to client satisfaction requires the rigorous and unrelenting pursuit of the core values of excellence, commitment and intensity," Jones says. "To build a preeminent client base, one must concentrate on excellence and value. The pursuit of consistent quality must be unyielding."

That Akins Gump has been able to sustain a high level of performance for 65 teams is a function of Jones' organizational skills. Computerized performance tracking, bi-weekly strategy meetings, standardized report forms and spread sheets form a knowledge management system that not only tracks performance, but spots both trouble spots and team opportunities.

With all the advantages to the firm from client services teams, the greatest beneficiary is the client. For the client, the program means more efficient service at lower overall cost, access to vast resources that might otherwise be difficult to draw from the firm, rapid response and better crisis management, and budget certainty.

For the firm it has meant improved client relations, high value and interesting work, and all of the advantages of the trusted advisor relationship. Significantly, it has also meant higher annual fees than ever before – from an average of $5.3 million from 1993 to 2001, increasing to an average $7.0 million from 2002-2004.

And where once attorneys were reluctant to collaborate with one another, the Akins Gump team members are more than enthusiastic. Says one partner in Dallas, "From simply communicating new developments to coordinating approaches on new opportunities, the client service team has been invaluable to maintaining our relationship in an increasingly competitive environment." Says a Washington, D.C. based partner, "The client service team approach has netted the firm energy, work, and litigation opportunities that we have not had in the past, and was an important factor in the firm's selection to be one of Deutsche Bank's eight preferred providers." And more of the same, from all of the partners functioning as part of client service teams.

The client service team is a 21st century answer to the dramatic changes in the professions and the clients they serve. It's a new structure for law firms – and accounting firms as well – to meet the client needs of the future in an era of elevated competition. It is a structure that enhances sensitivity to client needs, that allows firms and clients to become real partners, and that more than anything, offers real competitive advantage.

The well run team program is not a simple nor a casual concept. It requires the commitment of the partnership, and recognizing that new times call for new structures and views of professional practice. It demands the enthusiastic support of the firm's management team, a clearly developed and dedicated program, and the organizational skills of a client service coordinator who fully understands the client relationship process. It can be a complex program, and certainly, it must be done recognizing that it requires departure from traditional professional practice.

But when it works, it's worth its weight in successful and profitable client relations.

{Chapter 17}

Can David Beat Goliath Again?
Ten Things Small Firms Can Do To Compete

Great turbulence in the accounting profession, as well as in the business world itself, make these difficult and unusual times. Public outcry against the misdeeds of a few accounting firms, corporations, investment bankers and others in government and the business community is tarring the innocent as well as the guilty. In the meantime, the loss of Arthur Andersen and the consolidation of the now Big Five can alter the competitive landscape for firms of any size. It's likely that the major firms will accelerate a long standing practice of reaching into the low end of the market – the very market of the smaller firms. For the smaller firm, competition will come from unaccustomed quarters.

Can the small accounting or law firm successfully compete? History says yes, if the firm follows at least some of the following points...

- **Don't be sanguine about the health of your firm.** You may feel that you're in good shape today, that you have a substantial share of a specific industry, that your reputation will sustain you from assault by competitors, that you are immune from competition. In a rapidly changing world, this is when you are most vulnerable. Changing economic conditions, new regulations, an undercurrent of skepticism about the professions that, unwarranted as it may be, is still fostered by the Arthur Andersen situation – all these and more require that you be ever alert in your marketplace.

- **Save your current clients.** Your current client base is your first line of defense in a highly competitive environment, in which your best clients are coveted by larger firms. Examine your work with each client frequently, to assure that you are satisfactorily meeting your client's current needs. Be sure you understand the client's industry as well as his or her business. Be sure your person to person relationship is in good shape. And above all, pay strict attention to the quality of your own work.

- **Seek new business from existing clients.** In the average mid-sized firm, there should be a 20% annual growth in business from existing clients, even in slow economic times. This is accomplished by frequent conversations with the client about his or her business (not yours.) In any in-depth discussion about the client's business, if you listen carefully you're likely to hear some new problem about which you can say, *"I can help you with that."* Remember, your client's business may not be static, but instead, changing as the client's own markets and business change. Without a client relationship that keeps you in touch, you can depend upon two things – that your business for that client will remain static, and that sooner or later somebody will hold that discussion, and you'll lose the client.

- **Organize for productivity.** The future, in difficult times, lies with the lean, mean machine. That's the one with full control of process, expenditures and business practices. Don't be afraid, though, to invest in technology that works for you, such as extranets that tie your system to your clients, or the social media. Be sure your technology is equal in capability to your clients', and compatible in ways that count. Manage your firm for profit first, and comfort second. If you're profitable, you'll be comfortable.

- **Focus on business.** Know what business you're in, and carefully consider any changes in your business model or the services you offer. Know what skills you have, and work to sharpen them. In these times of changing regulation and technology, continuing professional education is a necessity, not a luxury. The competitive edge is not necessarily very large, but is rather an incremental edge.

- **Modify your culture.** For generations, the accounting and legal professions have always relied on a concept of professionalism that was rooted in the fact that, as professionals, the clients needed the professions more than the other way around. After all, nobody wakes up in the morning and says, *"What I really need today is a good audit."* Or *"What a great day to sue somebody."* Business comes to accountants because it has to. The accountant keeps the books in an orderly manner. The lawyer defends and protects in all legal actions. The accountant audits the company because the government or a lender or the company's investors demand it. But is your firm always the one that business comes to for these professional services? Or does it go to your competitors? Today, the demand is for more competitive services, and for services that not only attest, but help. This means that to compete, the culture of the professional firm must shift from an abstract professionalism to an aggressive market-centered orientation. Once, before the *Bates* decision that eliminated the strictures on professional firm marketing, firms could rely on their professionalism alone to attract clients. Not today. With competition being served by sophisticated marketers and marketing methods, the option to market is gone. To survive, compete. To compete, change the firm culture to serve the demands of competition.

- **Market.** Your survival in this new environment depends upon your understanding and using the skills of professional services marketing. Marketing is itself a profession, and marketing an accounting or law firm is very different from marketing a product. But while the professional marketer has skills and experience that are not necessarily within the realm of the professional's own experience and skills, there is still a great deal you can learn to do. Certainly, you should know enough to allow you to deal comfortably with a professional marketer. You should know how to define the market for your services. You should know how to look at your firm and services in terms of the needs of that market. You should understand the tools and vehicles of marketing that are needed to project your services and capabilities to your market. You should know how to manage the effort, even if it's done by professional marketers. And should you believe that the need for you to market is precluded by your current success or your reputation, realize that you've lost the option to market or not, simply because your competitors are doing it... and they are after your clients and prospective clients.

- **Challenge yourself.** Today's business world is more dynamic than ever before. More innovation, more competition, globalization that touches even the smallest firm – all demand more of the accountant. The successful accountant today is the one who constantly searches for new ways to meet the new challenges. The successful accountant, in today's environment, is the one who demands more of him or herself. Ask the question – as frequently as possible – *"This is the way I did it yesterday. Is there a better way, or a good reason, to do it differently today?* "This is a sure fire way to keep from getting stale, and to keep your clients from going to someone else who isn't.

- **Learn.** Continuing education programs are important and necessary to keep up with changes in the skills of professionals and the new regulations and laws that affect the profession. But the world of the professional accountant is no longer limited by just the skills of the profession. Today's successful professional understands more about business, about government, about globalization, about technology, about relationships, than was necessary in the past. Today's successful professional is an individual well aware of the larger world in which he or she functions, and is constantly learning about context, as well as skills.

- **Think increments.** A secret of success in business is to understand that to succeed, you don't have to be substantially better than your competitor. It takes only the smallest increment to be the best. A slightly better understanding of your market. An article or two more in your client's industry publications. A touch more visibility in your market place. A little bit more active in your networking organizations. It's amazing how little difference there is between firm number one and firm number two. If you think about that small difference you can make in your own practice, then you'll be number one in your area and market.

There may have been a time, once, when good enough was good enough for any accountant or lawyer. There may have been a time when just doing it as well today as you did it yesterday was enough. But in today's competitive world – a world of profound changes – that time is past. You have to be a better professional today to succeed in a highly competitive market.

{Chapter 18}

Don't Solve The Problem – Do A Brochure

On Being Original In A Brochure

There is a peculiar comfort in a brochure. It's easy to feel that if you've got one, you've taken care of marketing. Or most of it, at least.

Brochures, then, are too often done "...because everybody has one," rather than as part of a thoughtful marketing plan.

A brochure, in this context, is a pamphlet or booklet that describes a firm, a facility or a service. It may be used to explain all or a segment of the firm's services, or how the firm functions in a particular industry, or addresses a specific problem.

Despite the values inherent in well-done brochures, there are some pervasive misconceptions that substantially undermine their very real value to sound marketing. Perhaps the most expensive misconception is that brochures *sell* – that a prospective client will read a brochure loaded with glowing adjectives, and sign a contract as a result of it.

To assume, too, that people read brochures thoroughly and carefully is another trap. In fact, a brochure, no matter how attractive or thorough, is usually simply glanced at. It may be read in conjunction with other material, to get an overall impression of a firm. But it's rarely devoured like a novel.

There's a tendency to forget that publications strongly compete against one another – and against other marketing literature – for a prospective client's attention. Your brochure is rarely the lone voice in a wilderness. Nor can a brochure be merely self-serving, ignoring the needs of the reader. The brochure that sings the praises of oneself may fulfill egos, but rarely will it fill coffers.

For all that a good brochure can contribute to a marketing program, it's rarely the keystone of a total marketing effort, nor should it be. But as an *adjunct* to a marketing plan, it can be useful.

The Power of the Well-Designed Brochure
In conjunction with other marketing tools, brochures...

- Are tangible, with staying power. They give dimension and weight to anything you say about your firm and capabilities.

- Can demonstrate a firm's most valuable asset – its intellectual capital.

- Catalog and describe a firm's capabilities, facilities, expertise, or point of view, all in best light.

- Can supply valuable information, redounding to the benefit of the source.

- Give visual dimension to a firm. A well-designed, attractive publication implies a well-run, efficient organization.

- Give legitimacy to a new facility or service. A new practice in an existing firm, for example, becomes tangible to both its prospective clientele and the firm itself when it appears in print.

When Is a Brochure not Indicated?
A brochure is distinctly contraindicated when...

- It's not part of a plan that delineates why it's being done, and how it's going to be used.

- There is no clear view of how it will demonstrate the firm's intellectual capital.

- There are better ways to accomplish the objectives set for the brochure.

- It can't be done with a professional and businesslike appearance.

The Web Site

It's now difficult to think of a brochure without thinking in terms of a web site. The two are different, of course, although the inevitable question is that if you've got a web site to carry your information, why do you need a brochure? Several very good reasons…

- People have to come to a web site to see it. You put your brochure in the hands of the people you intend to see it. Serendipity is great, but you can't build a practice on it.

- A brochure is static. It stays what it is until you rewrite, redesign, and reprint it. Very expensive. A web site can be changed every ten minutes, if you like.

- You can't see a web site without a computer. You can read a brochure on the subway.

- The content is different. The web site is more dynamic, constantly changing (or at least, it should be), and constantly updated. Its strength is in its immediacy. A brochure's strength is in its constant, focused message.

And don't think that you can simply put your brochure on your web site. Nobody will look at your site a second time.

The Basic Questions

Within the context of even the simplest marketing program, thinking about brochures should begin with the very basic questions…

- Who is our audience, and what do we want them to know, think, or feel after they've read my publication?

- What are we trying to accomplish with this publication in terms of the overall marketing program?

- How will the brochure be used in conjunction with other marketing tools?

- Will some other marketing tool better accomplish what we want the brochure to do?

- How will the publication be delivered?

- Understand *positioning* – What is the one most important thing about your service that meets the most significant need of your prospective clientele? That position should be at the crux of your brochure – the guiding and impelling factor that drives the thrust of your brochure. (A classic example of how a position works was the sign in the war room during President Clinton's first election campaign – It's the economy stupid. It told the campaign staff that the economy was the primary concern of the electorate, and that every messaged, speech, or piece of literature must have that position as the driver.)

The answers to these questions will, in turn, focus the objectives of the brochure, and lead to developing a more effective document.

The format is dictated not by arbitrary choice, but by the role the brochure is to play in the marketing plan. Too often, the graphic designer is called in before the writer, and before the brochure's marketing role is defined. This subordinates the message to the design, almost invariably resulting in a visually attractive publication that diminishes or fails to serve the communications or marketing objective. In fact, be sure that the designer understands that the message is in the text, not the design. Let the text do its work.

Still, publications should be professionally designed, written and produced. Amateurism will say things about your firm that are unflattering and counterproductive. If appearance is not the primary factor, desktop publishing may be sufficient. But a brochure to rest on the desks of CEOs of prospective clients should not be home produced.

The art of writing a brochure is exactly that – an art. But in writing brochures for a law or accounting firm there are some distinct considerations that can make the difference between a brochure that accomplishes your objectives and one that doesn't.

The thoughtful, and most useful, brochure for a professional firm must solve a major problem – how do we describe our facilities and services in ways that differentiate us from our competitors, and at the same project quality? Ethics, of course, preclude comparison, which forecloses a classic marketing device.

One problem – one nagging problem – remains. How do you get the message across without using the same language that everybody else uses, and saying the same things that everybody else says? How do you distinguish one professional firm from another, when you can't use adjectives? No problem is more vexing than this.

That's the dilemma. With a product, you can make a distinction. You can make a claim, and maybe even prove that claim. "Our bulbs are brighter and last longer than their bulbs." Presumably, you can also say, "We do better audits," or "We do better briefs," but you can't prove it, and who'd believe it?

What Works?

The answer is always emerging, driven by the imagination of marketing professionals, but we do begin to see some things that work:

- Clarify the objectives. Again. Clarify the objectives.

- Think *positioning* – the guiding and impelling factor that drives the thrust of your brochure.

- Keep it simple. Don't try to say too much in one brochure. Make one point about your firm and make it well, and you're ahead of the game. Nobody, remember, reads a brochure like a novel, cover to cover. Let major points stand out for the skimmers. Go for the overall impression, and don't try to tell everything in one brochure.

- Focus. Limit the brochure to a single purpose. A service. A facility. A single problem and its solution. Omnibus brochures seem to be less effective than the single-purpose document. And always with the position in mind.

- Always have a plan to use the brochure effectively, before you start to write it. Know beforehand who your audience is to be. You have different things to say to different audiences. How you write anything is a function of who you're talking to, and no one statement is universal. Know how the brochure is to be distributed, publicized, used in both direct mail and personal selling situations. A brochure to be sent ahead has a very different point of view than one to be left behind following a meeting, as a summary or reminder, and to reinforce points made in person.

- Write about your solution or services as if you invented them, even if you know you didn't. It may be the first time your reader has seen that capability or solution delineated.

- The operative word, implied or in fact, is "you." Most brochures die when the first word is "we." Your brochure must be cast, invariably, in terms of the needs of the market – what the prospective client needs, not what you have to sell.

- Don't tell the reader what he or she should think about your firm – demonstrate it. Don't say, "We become involved with our clients' business," find a way to demonstrate it. Don't say, "We pride ourselves on service," find a way to demonstrate it.

- Don't expect the brochure to present an image – if by image you mean a perception of your firm that's other than reality. If you don't like the way your firm is perceived by the market, don't try to change the perception by manipulating symbols – it won't work. Rethink the business you're in, change the firm accordingly, and then write the brochure – not the other way around.

- Don't cast your brochure in stone. The life of a firm brochure shouldn't be more than two years. If your marketing program works, and your firm grows, it will outgrow the brochure in less than two years. If the brochure is applicable to the firm and still current after two years, then your firm is in trouble. Even if you don't want to be larger in two years than you are today, there's going to be some kind of change and growth. If it doesn't happen, you're in serious trouble as a professional and as a business.

- The best way to describe who you are isn't by describing it – why should anybody believe you? It's to demonstrate what you do, and how you do it differently. Use case histories. You don't have to use the client's name. You can always say, "A manufacturing company had an inventory problem arising from the vast number of small parts used in its product. Smith & Dale solved the problem by…" As the song goes, "Don't speak of love – show me." The trick is to talk about what you've done, not what you say you can do. "I can leap a wall a thousand feet high" is nothing compared to "Here's a picture of the high wall I leapt and here's a picture of me leaping it."

- Borrow from corporate annual reports. In the attempt to get the reader's attention, corporate annual reports use a number of exciting devices and techniques. A round table of financial analysts discussing the company. The CEO interviewed. An illustrated first person narrative. Boxes and sidebars to depart from the narrative to discuss an important point, or to define an unusual concept.

- Deliberately try to be different. If everybody else plays a major scale, play a minor scale. If you said it this way last time, say it that way next time. Do you want to be read? Work at it. Clichés don't work. If you can't do more than clichés, save your money. Don't do a brochure.

- Purpose alters the format and text of a publication.

- Think carefully about illustration. All professionals seated at desks look alike. Use both your own people and client situations imaginatively. Appropriate graphs and charts can help.

- Be thoughtful about details. For example, how a brochure is to be distributed affects it's physical design. If it's to be mass mailed, postage costs are a major consideration. Odd shapes that use custom designed envelopes increase costs substantially. Consider, too, how long the publication will be expected to do its job. A brochure with an intended long life shouldn't have dated references.

- Work with professionals. Sure it looks easy. You know what you want to say about your firm. You know how big you want the pictures to be. But as effortless as the better brochures look, that's how hard it was to get them to look effortless. Conceptualizing a brochure that really says to your clients and prospects what you want to say to them is an art form, rooted in skill and experience. Designing a brochure is a skill that's as professional as yours, and the difference between a brochure that's a chore to get through (and so won't be read) and one that's as inviting as a chocolate cake is artfulness. Use a professional.

The artfulness in a brochure is derived from knowing beforehand what you want people to know, think, or feel after they've read it. The art in a brochure is getting people to really read it in the first place, and to accept what they've read as news, as gospel, as a point of instruction and interest.

A brochure, in a sense, is no different from any marketing tool. Properly used, it works. Improperly used, it not only doesn't help, but it lulls you into thinking that you're accomplishing more than you really are. Better to take the larger view; to develop the larger marketing context in which the brochure is a working cog.

{Chapter 19}

Being Social In The
New World Of Social Media

Talking To Prospects When Prospects Can Talk Back

There are four things to know about what we now call the social media.

First, it's *media* – a means of communication, a medium, not of itself a magic carpet. Which means that its value lies in its ability to convey ideas and facts to a vast world of viewers. Which means, as well, that we're back to the old computer nostrum of "Garbage in-Garbage out." Or to paraphrase another (if contrarian) view, it's not the medium, it's the message.

Second, it substantially changes the world of marketing. In the old marketing, we talked to people who couldn't really talk back (other than by buying or not buying what we were selling). Very primitive and cumbersome. With social media, marketing becomes a conversation. We no longer talk at people, but with them, which creates a dynamic that never existed before. And what was once a mass market becomes an individual market, but one with individual feedback. For lawyers and accountants, who, by the definitions of professional services marketing, must participate in any marketing activities, this is a new and invaluable tool. It must be learned by the professionals who would compete with one another for practice development.

Third, it puts marketing directly in the hands of the professional – the lawyer and the accountant. I remember, back in the early days of the personal computer, when no lawyer or accountant would consider touching a typewriter keyboard (that's what secretaries were for). I remember, back then (1981), seeing a partner or two with the old Kaypro computer (an early version of a laptop computer), hidden under the desk. Today, no desk in any firm is without a desktop computer. Many of these desktops are now used by lawyers and accountants for Facebook, LinkedIn, Twitter, or managing blogs, as marketing tools. It is very much Marketing 3.0.

And fourth, today's social media define the meaning of change, which is the result of an evolutionary process. They went from non-existence to dominant communications devices in a relatively few years. The beauty of this is that the evolution Darwin spoke of was a process of incremental change over thousands of years. Moreover, unlike traditional evolution, which is driven in large measure by environmental response, social media are an evolution of an idea – an evolution of the mind. With the social media, it's a process that resulted in substantial change, in our lifetime. Darwin would love it.

Social media, in its various iterations, means computer applications such as Facebook, Twitter, LinkedIn, blogs, and the like. (*The Marcus Letter*, I should note, was one of the first professional services marketing sites that bestrides newsletters and blogs. In the evolutionary context, it began with my book, *Competing For Clients* in the 80s, which became *The Marcus Report* – a print version of a newsletter, which became the online *Marcus Letter*, which is still going strong.

Facebook and similar applications started in places like college dorms for on-campus socializing. They were quickly adapted as business tools for both marketing and client relations, many of which are now remarkably sophisticated. Business people, and especially marketers, quickly recognized their value for their feedback ability and sustaining relationships. What was once one way communication now became two way discussions – a new dimension in marketing and, for professionals, practice development.

As with any new technology, many books are being written on how to do it. Like so many books in this context, many are shallow and superficial. But two, while different from one another, are not.

Social Media Strategies for Professionals and their Firms, by Michelle Golden (John Wiley & Sons, Hoboken, NJ, 2010), is a comprehensive view and primer on the full range of social media, and of marketing specifically for professional services. Michelle Golden is a leading and nationally recognized expert in professional services marketing, as well as an experienced hand in the social media.

She writes for her market – lawyers and accountants – which she knows intimately. Professionals, she knows, tend to accept and adopt any tangible technology which, to them, means new equipment, like the late model smart phones that do everything. But they are frequently wary of new and unfamiliar applications of the equipment, like Facebook and Twitter. They involve social interaction in a marketing context that is not always within the ken or experience of professionals. Thus, the mechanics may be within their grasp, but not their uses in dealing with strangers, particularly on a large scale, such as marketing. And so the real problem she addresses in her book goes well beyond simply how to access Facebook, LinkdIn, etc., but how to use them as working tools. How to use the tools to relate to a broader audience. The etiquette and ethics. And how to tame the dynamic of the new media. Thus, her book takes the reader step by step through the process. In her detailed discussion of LinkedIn, Twitter, Facebook, and blogs, her step-by-step discussion of each does a terrific job of taking the reader from neophyte to expert, from getting started to using each effectively in any context.

All this, and more, she does remarkably well.

Social media, she points out in the first chapter, "…is not strategy. Social media are plural, and individually or collectively, they are not strategies." Nor, she says, are they initiatives or tactics. She then defines the distinctions among the different values and purposes of the new media, all as a context for addressing the media themselves. It's a remarkable foundation – easily comprehensible, and a basis for discussing the different aspects of the services.

Golden carefully delineates the achievements of effective use of the social media, citing both the personal and firm advantages, including reputation, prospect identification, networking, recruiting, self-publishing, and customer relations. She explains how the media can be used to build credibility, and to enhance networking.

Nor does she ignore the evolution from the basic use of the computer to gather data to developing its uses today as a highly personalized communications and marketing tool. This is significant, because it offers a clue to the future of networking by computer, which, I think, is crucial to understand in developing its uses to the individual and to the firm. Neither does she ignore comparisons' between using social media as compared to the more traditional marketing approaches, describing the differences in such areas as tone, conversation, validation, reach and control. This is consequential to understand how best to use each medium – social or otherwise – in planning the marketing program.

And finally, she discusses the best online writing techniques, the etiquette, and the best practices. All, of course, with case histories.

This is a rare kind of book – one that assumes, at the outset, that the reader knows little or nothing about the subject, and without talking down, goes through it carefully and thoroughly. Michelle Golden's book can and will make a difference in the proficiency of those who will benefit the most from it – the lawyers, accountants, and the marketers who serve them.

Facebook Marketing, by Justin R. Levy (Que Publishing, Indianapolis) doesn't specifically address the marketing context of professional services, but is useful nevertheless as an overview of what to do and how to do it in Facebook. Its marketing principles are generally sound, if not always applicable to the arcane structures of professional services. It explores some of the large variety of applications for which Facebook is useful, and gives examples of how it's used in a number of contexts. It delineates the mechanics clearly and understandably, which can be particularly helpful for the non-technically experienced neophyte. The author is Director of Business Development, Marketing, and Client Relations at New Market Labs, and writes with authority on the subject, but the book bespeaks no knowledge of the unique qualities of professional services marketing.

As for the future of social media, no one can say – simply because it's still a work in progress, too often in unskilled hands. It's got a toe in the future, but it would be foolish to say it's there yet. Ironically, good books – hard copy – will help.

{Chapter 20}

I Caught It – Can I Keep It?

Keeping Your Client Out Of The Competitive Pool

The conventional wisdom is that it costs more to get a new client than to keep an old one. And for once, the conventional wisdom is correct.

Yet, many professionals too readily take clients for granted. Or don't look for opportunities to increase revenues from perfectly satisfied clients.

Then there's the classic story of the client who went to another firm for a particular service. "Why didn't you come to me for that service?"

" Because I didn't know you did it." It happens too often.

Some firms have full-scale client retention programs. Some firms simply have a philosophy about clients – a point of view that says that new business is terrific, but "our business is built on our existing clients."

And on the other hand, some firms don't seem to grasp the dynamic of client service. There's the story about the guy whose wife was suing him for divorce. "Judge, he never tells me that he loves me." And he answers, "I told you I love you when I married you. It holds good till I revoke it."

The reality is that this new world is competitive in ways that it's never been before. Ask your clients how many times they've been approached by your competitors, and pursued aggressively. And then ask yourself if you can continue to be sanguine about keeping your clients happy, on a day-by-day basis.

There are, of course, some things that are clearly necessary in client retention. Doing good work, obviously. Being responsive, obviously. Being timely in delivering promised reports and material. Being polite to clients.

But these are things that should be taken for granted – things inherent in the meaning of professional. It's what the client is paying for. You get no credit for doing them, but you lose clients for not doing them.

The larger picture of client retention, on the other hand, is predicated upon recognizing the competitive and changing nature of the marketplace. Sophisticated marketers have a strong handle on who their client company is, what the company does, what its needs are, and how to address those needs in marketing approaches.

Which means that if you don't have that same knowledge, and the kind of relationship that means total involvement in the client's concerns, then you're in danger of losing that client.

Client retention, then, requires more than the obvious factors of doing good work and delivering it on time. And in fact, in a dynamic business world, it's often more than a personal relationship. It's at least…

- **Being immersed in a client's business and industry.** While the professional has a stake in some aspects of arm's length relationship, this doesn't preclude knowing enough about a client's business to anticipate problems in your professional area, and to seek new ways in which other of your services can help the client.

- **Frequent contact points,** beyond the engagement. You do, of course, what you've been hired to do. But you help both the client and yourself when you send a brochure on a subject of mutual interest. Or a copy of a clipping in which you've been quoted on a subject the client might care about. Or a simple newsletter, either your own or one of the excellent packaged ones, covering information of interest or concern to the client. The client should know you exist between contracts, between matters, between consultations.

- **Maintaining personal relationships.** Not just drinking and dining to keep the client happy, but establishing and reinforcing a sense of mutual understanding and trust. The degree to which the client calls on you for business advice is as much a matter of personal trust as it is professional trust.

- **Visible quality control systems.** You may have your internal quality control systems, but if the client doesn't know that, then the client has no reason to believe they exist. More importantly, the quality control systems should relate to the client's business, not yours.

Quality, a buzzword frequently used in business, relates to the client, not the professional firm. If the client doesn't perceive quality in terms of the client's needs, then your service can be the best there is, but not for that client.

The *client-driven*, rather than the *practice-driven*, firm is the only safe way to compete in today's market. Recently a major accounting firm took a highly conservative position on a matter pertaining to a client's problem. The problem was not the position, but that the position was taken for the law firm's protection, and not the client's – and the client was made aware of this.

- **Needs change.** Your services change. By constantly reviewing the client's needs, you not only assure that you're giving the client the best service, and that you're maximizing the relationship, but you're also telling the client that you're concerned.

- **Regular client surveys.** New York's former Mayor Koch used to walk the streets of the city, asking people, "How'm I doing?" He didn't always like what he heard, but he always knew. Anybody who doesn't take active steps to keep aware of client attitudes toward the firm is somebody who likes surprises. A simple one-page survey, annually, goes a long way.

Successful professionals are those who've learned the difference between *client relations* and *client service*. Both are important, but one is not the substitute for the other. In client retention, you have to have both.

It's the peculiar nature of professional services that quality plays little or no role in getting new business, except perhaps in terms of reputation. It plays a crucial role in client retention, on the other hand, if you define quality as giving the client what the client needs, wants, and expects. Most frequently, in order to know what the client needs, wants, and expects, you have to be immersed in the relationship. And you have to ask. Here, *quality* is not an abstraction – it's a reality.

Those who are most successful at client retention are those who actively work at it. They have programs and checklists. Even small firms that are aware of the need for it have programs that focus on paying attention. They listen. They contact. They understand the economics, and know what kind of return they're getting on their investment in it.

And they know, at first hand, why it's true that keeping a client is still cheaper than getting a new one.

{Chapter 21}

Advertising As A Marketing Tool That Sometimes Works

And Why It Sometimes Doesn't

Advertising, in professional services, has a strange history. More words, and more dollars, have been wasted on it, and less seems to have been learned from its mistakes than from any other marketing tool we currently use.

In the early days – the few years post-*Bates* (1977) – advertising was still anathema to law and accounting firms. Arthur Young was probably the first to do it after *Bates*, which was an exercise in courage (I was there – I remember) and then came Deloitte's *Beyond the Bottom Line* campaign. The more likely scenario at the time was typified by the then-managing partner of Price Waterhouse, who said about advertising, "Over my dead body." Now law and accounting firms, including its successor firm, PWC, spend millions. Marketing for professionals, as we know it today, didn't come easy. I'm not so sure it's much easier today. Certainly, getting it right in advertising is no slam dunk.

Unfortunately, advertising is much more complex than it looks. It is the most subtle of all marketing tools, and the most frustrating. It can even succeed by breaking traditional advertising rules, if that's done properly, by experienced copy writers, and with great skill and courage. But judging from the full body of professional services advertising, even most ad agencies don't seem to understand the differences between selling a law or accounting firm and selling toothpaste. And therein lies the core of the problem in most professional services marketing as its too often done today.

Why Advertise
Advertising has four major generic purposes:

- To inform, and to reinforce that information

- To create an umbrella of favorable attitude toward you and your firm (or product) – to pre-sell

- To open a prospective client's door to allow a personal presentation

- To either generate action (such as selling a product), or, in most professional services advertising, to allow for a more favorable context in which other action may comfortably take place, such as setting the stage for selling

- To focus internal priorities and appropriate actions

As more firms now advertise, it becomes increasingly important that the advertiser – the lawyer or accountant – as well as the advertising agency, understand the process as it pertains to professional services. To be passive in the process, and to allow a clueless agency to guide the decision, is as dangerous as eating unidentified mushrooms, simply because advertising is so different for professionals than it is for products. Your agency may be a good one, but if they don't understand that difference, then your ad may be clever, and attractive, but irrelevant.

It should not be forgotten that professional services are probably the only enterprises that depend upon the full participation of the professionals themselves for their marketing efforts. Product marketing doesn't often involve the people who make the product. But who hires a lawyer or an accountant without actually meeting the practitioner? How can an ad be written without input from the lawyer or accountant? In other words, ads alone don't do the job. A total marketing program that actively includes the professional does.

What, then, is the specific purpose of law and accounting firm advertising? *To build a reputation and name recognition that reinforces other marketing efforts that attracts and sells to prospective clients.* What's its role in professional services marketing?

This seems hard for product advertising people to understand, which is why most professional services advertising is so bad. Few people read an ad by a law or accounting firm and call up to say," I saw your ad – let's start Monday". Advertising builds an impression of the firm (which is why attempts to be funny are silly), name recognition, and reputation – *so that somebody who eventually needs a firm will tend to choose that of the better known advertiser rather than to choose the competitors.* If the ads address a specific problem or specialization, they are likely to get inquiries. Ultimately, it can be a significant element of a total marketing program – but without the full program the ads are doing only a fraction of the marketing job.

In fact, there is an unpleasant little secret. If you ran a series of ads that simply said, *"Smith & Dale is a law firm",* and ran it often enough, people would know your name. But you would be competing against firms with ads like the Ogletree Deakins ad (see Chapter 22), which goes beyond name recognition to project a capability and a quality sufficient to bring the firm to mind when people are choosing a firm for their specific needs, for your skills, and experience.

Some things to consider, then. Not rules – advertising is an art form, and frequently, the best advertising (and art) comes from breaking rules. But artists know that to effectively break the rules, you have to know what the rules are. Just some basics, then, to clear the way for originality, relevance, and effective advertising to function. (A paradox –fairness dictates noting that, through some anomaly or another, bad ads sometimes seem to pull or impress readers better than good ads. But that's part of the mystery of advertising.)

- Understand that with great advertising you can sell a product to somebody who hadn't known that product existed, but you can't persuade somebody to litigate or write a contract or have an audit unless the need for these services already exists. This is a major point. It dictates that the purpose of professional services advertising is primarily to get somebody who needs a lawyer or accountant to choose your firm rather than another one. Are there exceptions? Sure. If you're advertising to people who are part of a class and didn't know it. Or to people who might not know that their financial statements can be used to help them plan for their business. But these exceptions are the smallest part of the marketing for accounting or law firms.

- An advertising campaign is not a marketing program, and advertising rarely works except as part of a larger program that culminates in getting through the prospect's front door, and to the opportunity to sell.

- Remember that the nature of professional services marketing makes it difficult to judge the effectiveness of an ad or ad campaign in the near term. If I advertise toothpaste for sale, I know how effective the ad is by the number of tubes of toothpaste I sell. If I advertise, for example, a matrimonial practice, there is no such direct cause and effect relationship. I can persuade you to buy my brand of toothpaste with sound advertising, but with the best of advertising, I can't persuade a happily married couple to get a divorce unless they are actually considering divorce.

- In product marketing, company counts, as well as the product. There may be a thousand people behind the manufacture of a tube of toothpaste, but the interface between that thousand people and the consumer is the tube of toothpaste. The interface between a law or accounting firm and the client is the individual lawyer or accountant serving the client. Thus, the expertise you're selling resides in individuals, not firms.

- You can say, "My toothpaste is better than their toothpaste," But you can't say "We write better briefs," or "We do better audits." Not just because of any bar association rules, but because it isn't credible You can't prove it. And in any firm of more than two accountants or lawyers, some will be better than others. This is the "Sez you" factor. Absolute parallel consistency in legal or accounting skills is not likely – if not impossible. You can have consistency and quality control in a toothpaste factory, but not in a professional firm.

- It's pointless to announce that you do the very things you're supposed to do. *"Quality is important here." "Client service is paramount to us."*

"The client comes first." These are gratuitous statements and a waste of literary breath. They lack credibility, and do nothing to distinguish you from your competitors. Besides, they are the kind of factors that are presumably inherent in the professional practice.

- A cardinal mistake is trying to tell the reader what to think, or how the reader should think about you. Give them the facts that lead them to the conclusion you want them to reach, and if they can easily draw the conclusion you want them to reach, you've won.

- Don't misrepresent. The acoustics of the marketplace call catch you.

- And lose the concept of *image*, because, as the old saying goes, what you are speaks so loud I can't hear what you say you are. You don't change the way you are perceived by manipulating symbols. The symbols will be overwhelmed by truth.

- Differentiation isn't easy. But unlike product advertising, in which you can delineate points of a product's uniqueness or superiority, the best way to do it in professional services advertising and still be credible is to focus on the experience and expertise of individuals. See the Jefferson Wells and Ogletree ads. There are exceptions, but that's a good starting point. There are no easy ways to credibly differentiate one professional firm from another. The best you can credibly do is to demonstrate the realm of a firm's experience and expertise. Not differentiation in the same degree as in product advertising, this approach does something better – it distinguishes a firm, and that's better than tortured attempts at differentiation.

- In professional services advertising, or in any collateral publications, illustration is particularly difficult. You can't show a product, nor a factory. What seems to be left is an irrelevant stock photo of people at desks (yawn), or characters walking up or down courtroom steps. But then, there's ingenuity. Real people from your firm (see the Jefferson Wells ads) or metaphorical illustration (see the Winston and Strawn ad). As the noted legal advertising expert, Janet Stanton, points out, it's not just that the illustration should draw you into the ad, but that there should be relevance to the message and thrust of the ad.

- Corporate–type advertising rarely works in professional services. Generally, corporate advertising is when IBM says "Computing is good for you, and IBM is in the computing business." The difficulty with corporate advertising in professional services firms is that firms don't serve clients – individual lawyers or accountants or specialized teams do. But if Smith and Dale advertises that accounting is important for your business and they're in the accounting business, it helps with name recognition, but it doesn't say much about why Smith and Dale is a firm that does accounting better than the firm you're now using, or even well enough to serve you. This kind of advertising is called *branding*, an unfortunate concept that confuses name recognition for branding's promise of consistent, high-value service. In professional services, branding, like Coca-Cola or IBM, is a myth. A major consideration here is the role of the firm in serving clients and the role of the individual lawyer or accountant.

- A classic example of a rare corporate style ad that works for a law firm is seen in an ad for Zuckerman Spaeder, a litigation boutique. The illustration shows a lion looking at a bird in a bird cage. The headline reads, *"There's a fine line in litigation between safe and sorry."* The copy reads *"The world's business leaders strengthen their defense with the litigators at Zuckerman Spaeder."* Beautiful. It doesn't say, *"We're better silver tongued devils in a court room than the other guys."* It makes no promises, other than by implication. And it has the endorsement, strongly implied, of "the world's business leaders." Its impact resides in its subtlety – in what the reader is led to believe, without being told what to believe.

- Name recognition is important, and may be the most valid reason to advertise. You should get at least name recognition from your advertising, and the rest is context for it. But if that's your objective, know it at the start, so that it's still sound advertising – intriguing, informative, enticing, and not just gussied up with rampant cleverness for its own sake.

- *Positioning*, in all advertising, is important (But so is understanding what positioning really is.) Positioning says we understand your needs, and we know how to serve those needs successfully. Positioning is *not* saying this is who we are and what we can do, regardless of your needs. It stems not from the point you want to make, but from those of your market's needs that you can serve. Proper positioning is crucial to successful and effective marketing, and especially advertising. Without a clear position as a foundation for any ad campaign, the only beneficiaries are the ad agency and the publication – not the advertiser.

- The danger in all advertising is agency ego – the tendency of an agency to write ads that are clever and pretty, but that ignore some deeply ingrained experience of what works and doesn't work. This is the kind of advertising that ignores the crucial question, "What do you want the reader to know, think, or feel after reading the ad?" It's the kind of advertising that thinks that there's no difference between selling a product and selling a professional service.

But if it's all that difficult to do well, and expensive (never mind the return on investment), why do it? Many good reasons. Advertising a professional service can…

- Help to establish a professional presence

- Establish and support name recognition

- Spread word of your existence, and to broadcast the name of your firm and the nature of the services you perform

- Convey a favorable impression of your services, and the way in which you perform those services

- Engender and support prestige

- Help increase market penetration

- Enhance and support a position in the market

- Clearly delineate a firm's attitude toward the way its services are delivered

- Help define and project specific marketing objectives, based on a realistic perception of your firm and its services.

- Develop a need for your firm's services in addressing specific problems, by appealing to either the intellect or the emotions.

- Build a favorable context in which you can use other marketing devices and methods to urge and inspire people to take action in retaining your services.

- Help sell some services

- Help to define a new service, *in the context of the problems it solves*

- Afford the opportunity to be persuasive, even within the limited context of professional advertising

- Focus on a client problem or opportunity, and define how your service can help to resolve that problem, or seize that opportunity, for a prospective client

- Reinforce, and be reinforced, by sound public relations – as well as other marketing tools – that are designed to build and enhance reputation, to inform, and to focus an accurate perception of your firm and its services.

- Build a foundation that can enhance the more active marketing functions.

- Strengthen internal pride and morale, by demonstrating to staff a visible, concerted effort to project the firm and its strengths to the public

And in the cold call, it helps take the chill off of ignorance about who you are and what you can do.

What Advertising Can't Do

To understand its effectiveness, it's equally important to know what advertising can't do. For example:

- Unlike product advertising, professional service advertising, in most cases, can't persuade people to buy legal or accounting services they don't need for business or personal reasons

- With the exception of direct mail, advertising can never limit itself to precisely the audience you want, and so a measure of it – and a measure of its cost – is always wasted. Under the best of circumstances, there is a great deal of slippage in reaching an audience, and certainly in the cost of reaching that audience.

- No ad can work entirely on its own and out of the context of a larger program. The degree to which any advertising works is in proportion to a larger marketing effort.

- It can't supply complete objectivity or credibility. It's your space or time and your message, and readers know it. Readers also know that because you say something doesn't necessarily make it and so, and so all ads tend to be read with a measure of skepticism.

- No ad can close a sale for you, particularly in professional services. The best that can happen is that an ad inspires your prospective client to inquire further of you, or even to send for descriptive material, but that's not the same thing as making a sale or signing a contract.

These same principles apply, in large measure, by the way, to web sites and social media.

Ads that Don't Work and Some that Do

Certainly, the current crop of ads tends to be better than the earlier ones, although we had such weirdies as *Accounting Is Our Passion*. (*Passion* is the current fad word). I thought passion to serve clients is more to be desired. How many words will be wasted to explain the link between their passion and their ability to meet your need?

Then there was *Financial Restructuring Without The Bitter Aftertaste*, for a law firm. The copy's ok, but the illustration of three executive with faces screwed up (presumably from the bitter aftertaste), looks as if they've been drinking doctored Kool-Aid. Pretty inviting, isn't it? A good rule is don't try to be funny in public until at least six strangers, none of whom is related to you, laugh at what you've written. Nothing sours an ad more than unfunny attempts at humor.

Another law firm had a picture of a maze on one side of the ad, with the title *Legalese* beneath it, and in the other side, a picture of a bright young lawyer (a real partner), and the caption, *Practical Advice*. The message is that you'll understand what the firm is trying to tell you. Surely, the firm has greater and more valuable expertise than that? Isn't being understood by clients a basic in the practice of law?

A more elegant and effective ad shows a large picture of a Go board, with both white and black stones. The caption says, *Finding The Right Balance Between Risk And Reward Isn't Easy. Working With Your Law Firm Should Be.* Good ad, but when they say, *At Winston & Strawn our focus is results* (huh?), they move right back into the realm of obvious, lazy and wasteful copy writing. Do they expect you to believe that other firms don't focus on results? That's missing the point. It also comes under the rubric of telling the reader what to think, without crafting the path that leads the reader to arrive at your intended conclusion. It comes under the "Sez you" category, which means, essentially, don't say it unless you can prove it. Complex, but more of that in a moment.

An ad for an accounting and consulting firm shows a New Yorker Magazine-type cartoon in which three men are standing in front of a desk, apparently being interviewed. One is very tall and gangly. One is a button-down business type. One is a bald little man, barely able to see above the desk. The caption reads, *Secretly, Dave suspected that only one of the consultants would really fit in with his team.* But which one? And the copy, which is headed *Need Deeper Understanding?*, gives no clue – nor does it in any obvious way link to the cartoon. Strange.

It's interesting to note that these ads no longer appear.

An ad agency that knows how to do it does the ads for Jefferson Wells, a finance and accounting firm. A big picture of a real person – full page. A caption – *Pragmatism shows.* The copy then goes on to describe the fact that the woman in the picture has tackled multiple Sarbanes-Oxley engagements in the past two years, and has had fifteen years of audit experience before that. This is a woman who obviously knows. The implication is clear – she brings experience and expertise and a pragmatic approach to your problems. Another best of show

Will advertising distinguish one firm from another? Not likely, unless, like Ogletree (See Chapter 22), it's advertising a specialty. Nor, I think, is it necessary. Just projecting a firm's capability effectively will make it more competitive, and that's enough. There are too many law and accounting firms who do essentially the same things to make it necessary to go beyond that.

The people who did the Ogletree and Jefferson Wells campaigns are rare.

Generally, ads for professional services fall into two categories –the story, and the boast.

The story ad describes a situation that demonstrates a distinguishing factor about a firm, or – without blatantly saying it – leads the reader to a point of understanding and the conclusion that's responsive to the important question, "What do you want the reader to know, think, or feel after reading the ad?" When this is accomplished, the ad is most likely to be successful. A good example of this is the Jefferson Wells ad. It's impossible to not be drawn into the ad's story, and to not grasp the firm's expertise.

The boast is the self serving ad that demands that you accept their claim, without offering proof. The *"...we focus on results"* is an example. Similar ads in this category are those that talk of a firm virtue as if it was exclusive to the firm. There has been a rash of ads that boast of speaking plain English instead of lawyerese, or practical advice, as if these were exclusive virtues. The problem with boast ads is that they tend to be seen as empty promises. They tell no credible story, and in fact, the firms may do better to simply advertise, *"We are lawyers (or accountants). We do good work."* (Sez you.)

Why do ads that seem well written sometimes not work? Because they miss these points of advertising. Because they attempt to merely translate somebody's idea of persuasive talk into the ad medium, which can sometimes be like wearing a tuxedo to the gym.

But a product ad, to use the jargon of the ad business, *pulls*. A professional service ad *informs*. It will be rare, and perhaps serendipitous, that somebody calls you and says *"I saw your ad and want to hire you."* It happens, but you can't build much of a practice on serendipity. Another significant difference.

How, then, do you measure results of a law or accounting firm ad campaign?

- If the campaign is part of a larger marketing program, which it should be, you'll ultimately see the effects in talking to prospective clients.

- Existing clients will also tell you, as either a complement or a criticism, whether or not the ads square with their experience. (Pay attention to clients.)

- Your staff – those people who are responsible for delivering on the promise the campaign makes – will tell you, loud and clear.

Ultimately, if the campaign is a good one, it will be because your marketing people understand the process, and will carry it through to other aspects of your marketing. This means your practice will grow, even though you may not be able to specifically credit any part of the program.

Advertising professional services is a humbling experience.

The Foundation for an Ad

At the same time, There are some basic advertising principles that are indigenous to all advertising.

- Know your market. Not only who your prospect is, but what kind of service your market really wants and needs and is willing to buy, and what kind of problems they'll look to you to resolve.

- Know your service, in terms of what the prospective client is willing to buy, not simply what you're offering to sell.

- Every ad campaign should begin with a stated objective. Again, "What do you want the reader to know, think, or feel after reading the ad?" The objectives are not general, they are specific to each firm, each campaign, each ad. They dictate that the copy, and all other elements of the ad, are focused and relevant.

- Obviously, truth is basic. You don't promise what you can't deliver.

- The purpose of a *headline* is to attract attention and to bring the reader to the ad. A headline that offers nothing to the reader in terms of either benefit or interest may effectively mask the cleverest ad, and one that's offering the most useful service.

- The *text* should spring from the headline, and follow through the promise it offers. It should explain and clarify the facts and claims. It should be a logical progression of ideas, covering all of the points you mean to cover, even if it's done only with an illustration.

- Copy can appeal to the intellect and reason, or it can appeal to the emotions, or it can do both.

- Writing is not the manipulation of words – it's the expression of ideas. Words, grammar and punctuation, are merely the tools and devices we use to express ideas most clearly. To think of copy as a configuration of words is the same as thinking of a symphony as a configuration of notes.

Ads work best when you clearly understand your market, and clearly understand how your service relates to the needs of that market.

A headline that offers nothing to the reader in terms of either benefit or interest may effectively mask the cleverest ad, and one that's offering the most useful service.

The *text* should spring from the headline, and follow through the promise it offers. It should explain and clarify the facts and claims.

The *illustration*, which should have some relevance to the text, or otherwise attract the reader to the text.

The ad usually ends with a logo and a signature for identification and impression, and sometimes also a slogan.

And again, every ad campaign, and every ad, should address the question, *"What do we want readers to know, think, or feel, after reading these ads?"*

Writing the Copy

The artistry of advertising lies in the ability to manipulate symbols and ideas in order to inform and persuade people. As in any art form, there are no rules that can guide you in doing this, except to list those factors that seem to work most consistently. And yet, remember, some of the most successful ads are those that violate the rules.

Two universally accepted axioms are that an ad must be simple, and it must look and sound as if it's worth paying attention to. And obviously, it must be complete – it must contain all the information you want to convey. These axioms – if indeed they are axioms – spring from the fact that few ads are successful when these rules are ignored. Beyond that, clarity is essential. No matter how an ad is written it must be understood and easy to read.

There are some other guidelines that professional copywriters also find useful:

- **Talk to the reader, the listener, or the viewer.** Don't announce, don't preach. And don't get carried away by words and lose sight of the message. *"You"* is better than *"We"*.

- **Write short sentences,** with easy and familiar words. You want the reader or listener to do the least possible work to get your message. Even when you're talking to very bright people, communication is of the essence, not language manipulation.

- **Don't waste words.** Whether you use three or a thousand words make sure each is exactly the one you need. You're not writing an insurance contract for lawyers. An ad is information and persuasion.

- **Use the present tense and the active voice** ("All professional copywriters have extensive experience in preparing material," rather than " … extensive experience in the preparation of material."). If you do want a formal style it should be deliberate, and you should have a clear idea of why you are using it.

- **Punctuate correctly.** Punctuate to help the reader, and not merely to follow specific rules. The less punctuation the better, within the bounds of clarity, but don't be afraid to use it if it helps the flow of an idea. Don't be afraid to use contractions and personal pronouns, just as you would in chatting informally with a prospect. After all, that's what you're trying to accomplish in your ad.

- **Watch out for clichés.** They turn some people off. More significantly, people don't hear them as they pass mindlessly off the tongue without bothering to visit the mind, and the point you're trying to make is lost. (Again, unless you're doing it deliberately.) To be enthusiastic and exciting is to be well along on the way to being interesting.

- **Humor is dangerous**, unless you're professionally funny. Nothing defeats an ad like unfunny – and usually irrelevant – ad copy.

Writing is not the manipulation of words – it's the expression of ideas. Words, grammar and punctuation, are merely the tools and devices we use to express ideas most clearly. To think of ad copy as a configuration of words is the same as thinking of a symphony as a configuration of notes.

Why do ads that seem well written sometimes not work? Because they miss these points of advertising. Because they attempt to merely translate somebody's idea of persuasive talk into the ad medium. Because they don't know that "You" is better than "We". Because they didn't bother to learn the market.

And because somebody didn't recognize that the art of advertising copywriting is not the art of literary writing. Different medium, different art form.

{Chapter 22}

Ogletree Deakins Gets It Right

Doing The Perfect Ad

At last, the perfect law firm ad campaign. Well, pretty much perfect. The 39-office , Atlanta-based law firm has been running an ad campaign that embodies every principle of good advertising.

The latest ad in the *Wall Street Journal* has a picture of a man in front of a crossroad sign as if he were choosing which fork to take. The headline, which is really a callout in the middle of the copy, is in larger type than the rest of the text, which says *"where you go now"* (lower case as is).

The text says. *"As companies look to the future, the need for service-focused labor and employment law firm with national breadth and local presence has never been more critical. That's why Ogletree Deakins helps you determine the best path to reach your future destination. where you go now (the nominal headline), and the best path to reach that destination. One of the nation's largest and most respected labor and employment law firms, Ogletree Deakins has 39 locations and serves half the Fortune 50. Learn more at www.OgletreeDeakins.com.*

Then the subhead *"Ogletree Deakins. NOW"*

Considering the squalid state of most professional service advertising, this is the best because…

- The illustration is not frivolous, but specifically relates to the message, which illustrations and headlines often do not.

- The text reflects the message delineated from both the illustration and the modest headlines.

- It breaks from tradition by not having a standard headline, but uses instead a breakout of headline size text. A clear demonstration that in all advertising, breaking traditional rules can be effective, if done imaginatively

- It addresses a single practice – labor law—rather than trying to sell the whole firm, which benefits equally well in this context

- The ad states the problem faced by its market clearly, before it talks of the solution and the firm's ability to solve the problem

- It sums up the firm's ability to help in one sentence, followed by a description of the firm in the next, followed by the *"39 locations and half the Fortune 50"*.

- The ad is not only credible, it makes its point without self-serving boasts.

- It is beautifully written, spare, doesn't shout, and best of all, uses the word "you", not "we".

According to the Ogletree marketing department, the ad was created by a former ad agency with guidance and input for the firm's Client Services Committee. The objective, they say, was to let readers know that they have a knowledgeable, reliable partner for any labor and employment issue a business may face. They have a deep and diverse marketing program that centers on client service, experience, and on actively providing practical legal knowledge on any labor and employment law topic. The program supports the claims of the ad, and includes client assessment surveys, seminar and events, e-alerts, webinars, public relations, and speaking and presenting opportunities. They run advertisements on a regular basis, targeting business news outlets, respective trade publications, as well as diversity publications.

All in all, a fine piece of work.

In the larger context of advertising, Ogletree's committed program seems to recognize that the purpose of law firm advertising, as opposed to product advertising, is to build name recognition and reputation, which cannot be done effectively with infrequent ads. The problem with most law and accounting firm advertising is that it tries to create clients with its ads, which it rarely does. Who hires a lawyer or accountant from an ad?

In fact, there is an unpleasant little secret. If you ran a series of ads that simply said, *"Smith & Dale is a law firm"*, and ran it often enough, people would know your name. But you would be competing against firms with ads like the Ogletree Deakens ad, which goes beyond name recognition to project a capability and a quality sufficient to bring the firm to mind when people are choosing a firm for your specific needs, skills, and experience. But the Ogletree ad so focused on the reader and the skills that it can stand up to any other competitive ad.

Another case in point that illustrates another kind of advertising that's popular is another Wall Street Journal ad by Marcum – an accounting firm. There is no illustration, but the headline reads *"Discover the Marcum Difference."* In a grey box beneath the headline is a list of the purported firm virtues... *Integrity, Value, Discipline Excellence, Client Service, and Experience* (repeated a second time, with an asterisk that says It's that important to us). Below, on a white background, and the words, *"At Marcum, we've been putting our experience to work for more than 55 years. Our skilled professionals... etc."*

This is a generic ad that could apply to almost any other accounting firm. If there is some other objective in the ad other than marketing, it doesn't come clear. The virtues they list are part of every CPA firm's practice – if not, they quickly lose clients, if not their license. Are they implying that other CPA firms don't have integrity, value, client services, and so forth? And it's all *"we"*. You don't get to the *"you"* until the very last sentence in the ad – if anybody reads that far. Furthermore, it doesn't trust the reader to recognize those virtues. It doesn't delineate what the firm actually does and how it does it, nor does it in any way demonstrate the difference that the headline promises. And worst of all, it tries to tell the reader what to think, instead of demonstrating it to lead the reader to his or her own conclusions in favor of the advertiser. I call this egocentric advertising, because it tends to make the advertiser more comfortable about the ad and the firm than it does the reader.

There is a web site listed at the bottom of the ad, but no reason in the ad to go there. Too bad. The site is pretty good, although even at the site, there's too much "*we*" and not enough "*you*".

Now, if this is the only ad they run, it may impress their current clients, but not likely anybody else. If it runs only once or twice, even the name will be forgotten very quickly.

In view of my long-held principle that no ad should be judged without determining the advertiser's objective, I interviewed Bruce Ditman, Marcum's chief marketing officer. He explained to me that there is a larger advertising plan, of which this is the first stage. The objective? Name recognition, as I had suspected. But such an elaborate and expensive campaign? Because Marcum, an East coast firm, had grown recently by merging with several firms, including a presence on the West Coast, where the name was not known. By repeating the ad several times it was anticipated that the name would be recognized sufficiently to make the market more susceptible to marketing and client development activities.

As for the copy theme, it was meant to serve as a mission statement, Ditman said, as much for the staffs of the newly merged firms as for the public.

These are, on the face of it, valid objectives. However, I see it as a wasted opportunity to display the firm's specialties and skills, which would still accomplish their objectives. This, said Ditman, they plan to do in the next round of advertising.

My suspicion is that the people who did the ad come from a product advertising background, and miss the nuances of professional services advertising.

I should note, however, subsequent ads in the series attempted to enlarge on the themes of experience, but still dealt in generics, and still talked more about "*we*" than "*you*". Wasted opportunity, I think.

Another problem is that they may never know if there is a return on the investment – not, at least, in the near term. This is the curse of a great deal of professional service advertising.

What, then, is the purpose of law and accounting firm advertising? To build a reputation and name recognition that reinforces other marketing efforts to attract and sell clients. This is a hard lesson for product advertising people to understand, which is why most professional services advertising is so bad. Few people read an ad by a law or accounting firm and call up to say," I saw your ad – let's start Monday" advertising builds an impression of the firm (which is why attempts to be funny are silly), name recognition, and reputation – so that somebody who eventually needs a firm will tend to choose that of the better known advertiser rather than to the competitors. If, like the Ogletree ad, it addresses a specific problem or specialization, it is likely to get inquiries. Ultimately, it can be a significant element of a total marketing program – without which it's doing only a fraction of the marketing job.

It should not be forgotten that professional services are probably the only enterprises that depend upon the full participation of the professionals themselves for their marketing efforts. Product marketing doesn't involve the people who make the product. Who hires a lawyer or an accountant without actually meeting the practitioner? In other words, ads alone don't do the job. A total marketing program – including selling – does.

Will advertising distinguish one firm from another? Not likely, unless, like Ogletree, it's advertising a specialty. Nor, I think, is it necessary. Just projecting a firm's capability effectively will make it more competitive, and that's enough. There are too many law and accounting firms that do essentially the same things to make it necessary to go beyond that.

Unfortunately, advertising is much more complex than it looks. It is the most subtle of all marketing tools, and the most frustrating. It can even succeed by breaking traditional advertising rules, if that's done properly. Judging from the full body of professional services advertising, even most ad agencies don't seem to understand the differences between selling a law or accounting firm and selling toothpaste.

The people who did the Ogletree campaign are rare.

{Chapter 23}

There's A Leak In My Firm

Never Mind Who – Why?

OK, somebody talked to the press, and leaked information that shouldn't have been leaked. That's three problems, not one.

Primary, of course, is how do we control the damage caused by the leak. Then we worry about who did it.

The second problem is that who did it is frequently not as important as why it was done. That may be the more urgent damage to control. The problem caused by the press leak will go away by itself, most often. It has to be treated like any bad story, and we've talked a lot about that in *The Marcus Letter*. But the reason for the leak can be more stubborn to deal with, as is the mechanics of preventing leaks.

The mechanics of preventing leaks can be tricky, and that's the third problem. If they're mishandled, they can cause more damage to the firm than the leaks do.

Leak prevention, on the face of it, can be pretty obvious. For example…

- With sensitive information, limit access to only those who have to know. Chances are you'll find that it's fewer people than you think.

- Number and control sensitive documents, so that one person knows who has what documents.

- If you have a lot of sensitive information, appoint a security officer, even a temporary one, if that's what the situation warrants, with the responsibility to keep aware of who knows what and who has what documents.

- The greater danger in leaks is not the information that gets out – it's the effect of a climate of suspicion in the firm. Morale gets shot and efficiency goes way down when everybody functions under a cloud of suspicion. That's why the fact of the leak itself, and not the information leaked, is the more dangerous.

- This is not to say that the information leaked isn't damaging. It can be all out destructive. The leak about the partner's dissatisfaction with the managing partner, or the new merger can be devastating. The leak about merger discussions can wreck the discussions. But the damage done to a firm by the fallout from a cloud of suspicion can be the worst of all.

- If it persists, and continues to be serious, then get professional help. Detective work is no game for amateurs. Yes, you can play at it with such devices as feeding individuals deliberately false or marked information. Then if it leaks you know who did it. But this can be a dangerous game, with farther reaching consequences than you want. Get a professional on it.

Why People Leak Inside Information

It may be more important to find out why the information leaked. Except to punish the individual – which may not always be warranted – the leak is really a symptom. People leak information for several reasons…

- **Malice.** Some individual wants to cause damage, either for its own sake, or for revenge for some real or imagined slight, or for some other purely neurotic reason – all of which may be the same thing.

- **Self-importance.** Being able to tell a reporter, "I know a secret." There is absolutely no reason to believe that because an individual has reached a position of importance, he or she is emotionally mature – is not an adolescent.

- **Politics.** At one firm, a group opposed to the managing partner used leaks as a tactic to embarrass him. It worked, by leading the press to do a story based on the rumors that had been leaked. Because the leakers were the more cooperative with the press, their point of view was the one that prevailed in the story.

- **To curry favor** with a reporter, by being the source of inside information.

- **Innocent accident.** Somebody tells something to somebody without realizing that he or she is leaking, or spreading a rumor. Or somebody loyal to the firm innocently tells somebody else thought to be trustworthy – but who really isn't.

It's this array of reasons for leaking that comprise the dangerous symptoms.

Why should there be a ground for malice in a firm? Is the management group aware of it? What's the cause of it? What must be done to eliminate it – or to eliminate the individual?

The self-important individual is usually easy to recognize. That individual should be identified, and kept from sensitive information, when possible.

Politics is almost impossible to deal with in a firm, particularly a large one. The only solution is absolutely wise management. OK, as Napoleon said, then give me lucky generals. But this kind of situation is a clue to a serious crisis in management. A poorly managed firm, one in which the callousness to the needs of the firm leads to hurting the firm for an individual or a group's political advantage, is in serious trouble.

As for the other causes, they are primarily emotional or careless, They can be dealt with only by taking steps to make a point of not just the secrecy, but the reasons for it. If leaks are a problem, then firm management may have to make a point of patiently explaining how the firm is hurt by it, and how that affects every individual, including the person responsible for the leak. Thoughtlessness and mindlessness are not tolerated in dealing with clients. Why should they be tolerated in dealing with the firm?

On the face of it, leaks are a communications – and therefore a marketing – problem. But clearly, they are more than that, and should be treated accordingly.

The problem is that a leak in a firm is like a thief in the firm. It angers, beclouds, and saddens everybody. And everybody loses.

{Chapter 24}

Be Nice To The Journalists

Or Else You'll Turn Into A Pumpkin – Or Something

Your mother raised you to be nice to everyone, and you've always been taught to be nice to journalists. Answer their questions. Tell them everything. Stop what you're doing and cooperate. Be polite.

That's the conventional wisdom. You've even read that in *The Marcus Letter*. But are there ever times to tell the press to bug off, and leave you alone? Maybe.

On the face of it, the media seems to have all the power. They speak to a lot more people than you do, and they do it with what the general public accepts, usually unquestioningly and with little reason, as objectivity.

Trade lore abounds with stories of a journalist spurned. Back in the days of the famous columnist Walter Winchell, any celebrity – or press agent – who didn't cooperate with him might have done well to buy a grocery store for a new career. One press agent who promised him an exclusive, only to find that another columnist had inadvertently submitted the same story, was driven from her otherwise successful career.

Virtually every company, and every marketing or public relations executive, has a story of being trashed by the press – sometimes despite following all the rules and cooperating extensively.

But then, there are stories of companies that refused to deal with segments of the press, and are still around. Mobil – now Exxon/Mobil refused to talk to *Wall Street Journal* reporters for years. There is no empty crater where Mobil once was; they still thrive.

There may indeed be times, then, when being cooperative with the press is not the best thing you can do for your firm.

If you're dealing with a hostile journalist or publication, and believe you're in a no-win situation, you may have more to gain than to lose by refusing to cooperate.

If you're dealing with a publication whose editor thinks it's more important than it really is, and you know you're not going to get a fair shake anyway, why waste your time?

If you're asked to comment about a competitor, or about a situation in your industry to which you're ancillary, and there's any chance that your comment may be misinterpreted or even misreported, "no comment" is a great response.

There are many comparable situations, but they all add up to one thing – blind obedience to all rules, particularly the rules of marketing, doesn't always make sense.

The rules of media relations aside, the governing factor should be the well-being of your firm. There are values to public relations, obviously, and there are times when, despite the negative aspect of the story, you have an obligation to tell your side. But not always, and not universally.

Frequently, the press will trash a company. A few years ago, a major public relations firm took a beating on the front page of a major newspaper. Conventional wisdom at the time was that because of the story and the place in which it appeared, the firm was through. It didn't happen that way.

After a flurry of trade discussion, and possibly the loss of a potential client or two (no current clients were lost), the firm continued to thrive. Why? Because one story, positive or negative, doesn't have much effect. Only an ongoing campaign, positive or negative, has sustaining results.

So if you know that you're going to take a beating no matter what you say or do, or if you know that the reporter is unlettered or unknowledgeable in the subject and is only passing through the beat, or if you know that commenting is going to get you involved in something that may turn out to be flat, stale and unprofitable to you, then tell the media to bug off.

If you know that a reporter is misrepresenting to you what he's writing, in order to get your participation in a story that you might otherwise be reticent about, or if that reporter has done that to you in the past, you're perfectly right to decline.

In fact, participating in a roundup story should be done cautiously anyway, with you asking the reporter as many questions as he or she asks you. And if you do consider participating, take notes of what you're being told about the nature of the story. You may want to complain later.

The press has an inalienable right to pursue. They don't have an inalienable right to catch. There's a difference between being firm and declining and being rude. Rudeness is somebody else's game. Declining firmly and politely may very well be the way for you to win your game.

Your mother, then, may have been right. But not always.

{Chapter 25}

Spinning Out Of Control

When Bad Things Happen To Good Marketers

Every election campaign produces, among other things, media myths and bad language. During the elections of the last two decades, the language was infected by a new myth called *spin control*. The phrase, which broke a speed record in becoming a cliché after the 1988 election, implies that a good media relations practitioner can control the nature and texture of a story in the press – can put the right *spin* on it to get the journalist to tell it the spinner's way.

It's just not so. For all that the myth implies, when it comes to the media, we propose – but others dispose. Thus it was, and thus it always shall be, so long as we have a free press.

But is the telling always accurate? No. Is it always fair? No. Sometimes, despite all of the public relations professionalism, and despite all the cooperation we may offer the media, the story comes out badly. Disaster, dispensed in the aura of a supposedly objective media, doesn't merely strike, it reverberates.

The picture you so carefully and accurately painted is distorted, the wrong people are quoted and the right people are not, the facts are warped and bent beyond recognition, and the whole piece reads as if it were written by your most malicious competitor. Certainly, it will be relished by your every detractor.

The Experts' Advice

Beyond the first scream of outrage, what can you do? What has been done most effectively by others who have lived through it – and survived?

Perhaps the hardest factor of a negative story to deal with is that most people who are not professional marketers tend to overreact. At one extreme is incredible upset and anger; at the other is casual disdain that says, "So what, no one will believe it." Neither extreme is warranted nor accurate.

The most useful course, then, is to do nothing until you've recovered from your anger. Even doing the right thing in the wrong frame of mind can perpetuate, not cure, the damage. So…

- Don't act precipitously. Think of every action in terms of possible reaction. What seems like a good idea at the moment may backfire next week.

- After you've gotten over the emotional impact and the anger, don't think vindictively. You may have to live with that publication again someday, and vindictiveness in any event is not profitable.

- Assess real – not assumed or presumed – damage. That's where you've got to focus your attention. Much assumed damage at first light disappears when the sun comes up. What's left is damage you can deal with.

It's this last point that's crucial to successfully limiting the damage of bad press. Too often, the defense is predicated on imagined damage, in which case the reaction is an overreaction, and causes more damage than the original article.

Experts rarely concern themselves with why it happened. Unless libel is involved, it doesn't really matter. The reporter could have functioned out of ignorance or laziness. Reporters are people, and are not immune to such foibles as preconceived notions that can subvert the professionalism of even the most experienced journalist. There may have been an adverse chemical reaction to somebody in your firm, or a fight at the journalist's home that morning. It fact, it really doesn't matter, because the reason for an adverse story is rarely an element that can be dealt with in damage control.

There are some specific questions to be addressed:

- What does the article really say? Is it bad because it's wrong – or because it's right?

- Is the article distorted because the facts are wrong, or because they are put in a wrong context that distorts the facts?

- What is the real damage? Is it libelous? Misleading enough to cause real business damage? Or just embarrassing?

- Consider the publication. Is it widely read, or will people you care about never see it? (Consider that under certain circumstances, your competitor may want to make a point by sending a reprint of the article, along with a favorable one about himself from the same publication). What's the publication's reputation for credibility?

- Is the potential damage internal as well as external? Sometimes an unfavorable article can hurt internal morale more than it affects an external perception of the firm.

The Impact Fades Quickly

Staying power is an important consideration. How long after publication will the story, or at least it's negative aura, linger? Depending upon the publication and the nature of the story, considerably less time than you think. As one experienced marketer put it, the impact fades quickly, but the impression can linger.

Some time ago, a major professional firm was savaged in the press for nepotism. The impact was shocking. In fact, the firm not only lost very little business, but continued to grow. Did the story, on the other hand, contribute to competitive defeats? Hard to say. An impression may have lingered in a prospective client's mind, and contributed to other negatives. But ultimately, the damage was nowhere equal to the impact and shock of the article's first appearance.

Responding to the Damage

Assessing the damage accurately allows you to choose the appropriate response. There are, in fact, a number of responses, some, unfortunately, inappropriate. You can:

- Sue, but only if there is real libel and real – and demonstrable – damage. There rarely is.

- Get on the phone and scream at the editor. Good for your spleen, lousy for your future with at least that segment of the media. And you'll never win.

- Write a nasty letter to the publisher. Only slightly better than screaming, but with the same results.

On the other hand, there are some positive things that can be done:

- Avoid defensiveness. Plan positively.

- Warn people. If you know an article is going to appear that might be unfavorable, alert your own people, so that it doesn't come as a surprise.

- Have a plan and a policy, preferably before you need it. This should cover how to deal with the media, who does it and who doesn't, how to deal with client reactions, how to deal with internal reactions. It should cover how calls are handled, who responds and who routes calls to whom, what to say to clients and who says it, and so forth.

- A letter to the editor is important, if only to go on record. But it should be positive, non-vitriolic, and deal only with the facts. It should not sound petulant or defensive.

- Deal with the real damage. If the real damage is in specific markets, mount a positive public relations campaign aimed specifically at those markets. If the damage is internal, try to assess the root causes for the negative reaction. It would take a powerful article in a powerful journal to demoralize a firm that's otherwise sound and comfortable with itself.

- Consider how a competitor might use the piece, even within the bounds of propriety. It could be, for example, reprints to a particular market. Offset this with positive publicity to the same market.

No story is so bad that it should warrant extreme reaction. No publication that's still publishing is so devoid of credibility that some readers won't accept what they read. The role of the professional trained and experienced marketer is to maintain perspective, to assess the damage appropriately, and to see that the response is equal to – but does not exceed – the damage.

If bad press meant nothing, then neither would good press, and we know that consistently good press means a great deal. But one story – good or bad – rarely has sufficient impact to seriously aid or damage a company (although a negative story is more titillating than a positive one). Most positive public relations is a consistent series of positive articles, interviews and news stories. If a negative press consists of more than one story, then the problem is usually not the press – its the subject of the stories.

The perspective of the bad story, then, requires dealing with it as an anomaly. This means dealing with it as a calm and rational business decision. And no business decision, in any context, is ever a sound one if it isn't arrived at rationally and professionally.

{Chapter 26}

Same Game, Same Name, Different Rules

Any Old PR Person Will Do

There was a time when all you needed was a roll of nickels and a phone booth, and you were in the PR game. Of course, all clients expected then was that you get their names in the paper. For most of the publicity clients in those days, that was sufficient.

Those days were the late 1920s and 1930s, before PR became Public Relations, and before we were beset with such glorious concepts as *image*, and *positioning*, and *niche marketing*. Today, public relations is infinitely more sophisticated than that, as is the public relations client. The public relations program for any modern corporation is to its publicity ancestor as desktop publishing is to hieroglyphics. And of course, the public relations program for the professional firm is different, too.

But to have a sophisticated public relations program requires not just a sophisticated practitioner, but a sophisticated client. A firm, if it knows how, will always find a good public relations practitioner or consultant, but a consultant is only as capable as the firm he or she serves.

This is what's so fascinating about professional services marketing. By the 1970s, a great many product companies were very knowledgeable about public relations and what it could and couldn't do. That's the point at which lawyers and accountants and consultants, bright-eyed, eager, and suspicious as hell of this new marketing stuff, found themselves entering the arena.

Aside from the fact that professional marketers themselves had a lot to learn about what matters and works in professional services, and why a lot of what works in corporate public relations doesn't work in professional services, the professionals themselves had absolutely nothing to go on. And sometimes, even worse than inexperience or even ignorance, there was the mythology. You know, "We bought the guy lunch – why doesn't he print the story?" and "If we buy an ad will they run the story?" and "Public relations? That's free advertising, isn't it?"

The problem is that even the more than 20 years since *Bates* hasn't produced worlds of experience in dealing with outside public relations consultants. And while there are a great many accounting and law firms, and their outside public relations agencies, doing great work, there's still a good deal of groping. What does a professional firm do when it recognizes the need for – and value in – good public relations, but has never done it before? How do you know how to find, qualify, hire and monitor a public relations firm? How do you know how much to pay, and what you have a right to expect for your money?

There are several ways to answer that question. You can hire an independent marketing consultant with demonstrated expertise in the field to do an objective independent audit. The cost is minimal, considering the potential savings to you.

Or you can ask yourself the following questions.

- Does this firm have a background in either other professional services, or at least in financial services or corporate public relations? An ordinary product publicity firm, specializing in simply getting your name in the paper without a marketing context, just won't work for you, because your public relations program should address a point beyond just name recognition.

- Are the people who are going to work on your account smart enough to learn and understand the technical aspects of what you do, and why it might be newsworthy? Publicity for professionals most often hinges on being able to make technical subjects newsworthy.

- Does the consultant understand the larger marketing context, of which public relations is only one part, and how public relations fits into that larger context? If not, you may be in for a lopsided program that will leave you frustrated.

- Is the consultant clear in spelling out expectations for his or her program? If your expectations are not clear, then the consultant is doomed to failure, because you'll always expect more than the consultant can possibly deliver.

- The size of the consultant's firm doesn't matter – the thinking and ability of the person who will work for you do. There are some large and even famous public relations firms out there doing absolutely dreadful work (and some doing great work, of course), and charging vast fees. There are some very bright and energetic small firms that perform gloriously. In public relations for professional services, it's brains, not size, that matters.

- How much you should be paying a consultant is relatively easy to figure, these days. Organizations of both accounting and law firm marketers (AAM and LMA) have published surveys of costs. The range of fees is no different than the range of fees you charge – more for the most experienced, less for the less experienced. Check the fee structures in your area.

- References are extremely important. Ultimately, public relations is an art form. There are only a limited number of things that a practitioner can do, but how artfully they're done is what makes the difference. You'd find very little difference from one firm's proposal to another's – but a vast difference in references.

- How the firm reports is important. If they don't have a somewhat formal structure for keeping you informed, then there's a huge potential for mumbo jumbo reporting. There should be regular work sessions to give them input for their programs, but frequent status meetings as well.

- It should be the role of the public relations counsel to turn you from a naive to a sophisticated client, and you shouldn't hire any firm that doesn't offer to do that. There was a time when the client waited outside the door while the PR people on the inside performed their secret machinations. No more, and not in professional services, where the practitioner must be a partner in the marketing process. Hire the firm that understands that, and is willing to make you a part of the process. Eschew and forsake all others.

If once public relations people were fast talking hacks, those days are gone. There may be a flack or two hanging around the campus, but most public relations people today are smart, experienced, and knowledgeable. Those are the people you want working for you. Then public relations works for you.

{Chapter 27}

Where Went The 5 Ws?

The Press Release In Today's World

A recent business communication book says that in writing press releases, the lead paragraph should include the five Ws—*who, why, what, when, and where.*

A textbook on journalism written in the 1920s says the same thing – *the five Ws.*

Nothing has changed in more than 70 years? Don't believe it. Just read any good newspaper in the U.S., Canada, or Great Britain. And what newspapers do is what press releases must do. Why?

Because the simple press release, the staple of public relations, is not simple at all. It's a complex form of journalism, in which the press-release writer competes directly with the professional journalist, as well with every other press release sent at the same time, for scarce publication space or broadcast time.

All press releases compete in an arena in which the editor to whom the release is sent may not be particularly receptive.

The key to seeing your press release in print is to understand the journalistic process. This is very different from merely rewriting the last press release you read or wrote. In good journalistic writing, even if some of the *five Ws* are appropriately included, they're not the point. The point is to focus on the news itself.

There are other myths as well, such as always putting the least important news at the end, because that's the way editors cut. Not since 1910, if ever at all. That practice goes back to the days of the old telegraph, when less was more, because the telegrapher had to work at it. Now, newspaper editors are better and more professional than that. And with computers, clip and edit is out. It's usually all rewritten because with computers it's easy to do.

What do we see in a modern news story that can help us write better, more competitive press releases?

We see that the lead (or lede) paragraph is most often a terse, exciting summary of the heart of the story—a definition of its most important, intriguing, exciting elements Nor does it always attempt to tell it all in one sentence. The subsequent paragraphs then spell out the details, usually in descending order of probable interest to readers, and more significantly, relevance to the key elements of the lead sentence.

The first reader – the audience – of the press release is obviously not the newspaper's ultimate reader, but the publication's editor. If the editor isn't intrigued by the story—and by the first sentence—the release is dead. And don't rely on the headline you put on the press release. That's not what's always read. It's all in the first sentence, no matter what gems reside in the rest of the story.

The model, then, is not other press releases, but the news story itself. For example, this from the *New York Times*…

> *"In the race to commercialize new superconductors that could revolutionize the electronics, energy and transportation industries, the United States is already in danger of falling behind Japan, many experts say."*

In one exciting sentence, the writer tells the entire story, leaving only the details to be fleshed out. And without the traditional five Ws, the lead sentence defies the reader not to continue reading the rest of the story. Compare this with the more typical press release…

> *"Harold Adams, managing partner of the law firm XYZ, announced today that three new partners have been appointed."*

Does this release cause the editor to stop the presses and tear out the front page?

Who is Harold Adams? Who is the XYZ law firm, and why should anyone outside of the XYZ firm care? Of what interest is the appointment of three new partners to anybody except their families?

But suppose the lead were...

"New capabilities in copyright and patent law, litigation, and real estate law will now be available to local business, as a result of three new law firm partners appointed today by XYZ law firm, it was announced today by the firm's managing partner, Harold Adams."

Now the lead tells the editor that something significant has happened, which is more important than who it happened to. It may be well worth his time to read on to find out just how local business will be better served, and who these people are.

It's important to discern how each publication defines news because it tells you that you must cast even the most mundane story into one that dramatizes and excites (without hyperbole, of course). This is why reading a publication to determine its concept of news is crucial.

And even if your story is not likely to make the front page of the *New York Times*, by writing it as if it were, you are more likely to hit any publication you send it to.

In the final analysis, the release writer proposes, but the publication's editor disposes. Your only help, then, is skill in contemporary journalistic technique, and not in the release writing clichés of the past.

{Chapter 28}

Is More Publicity Better?

Or Is Better Publicity Better?

In the early days of publicity, when it was low-down press agentry and not high-blown public relations, the idea was to get your client's name in the paper. Often. In any context. Just spell it right.

In the early days of marketing professional services, it became clear that merely to get your firm's name in the paper, in any context, didn't help much. Ego, maybe, but nothing more. A new approach to publicity had to be developed.

What worked was to get individual firm members' names quoted in a context of expertise. *"You can save a million dollars on estate taxes," according to John Smith of Smith & Dale, "by..."* Or, *"The party liable for your accident may be the person you'd least expect..." according to Harry Writ, of Writ & Writ.*

This, in conjunction with such valuable activities as by-line articles and interviews on consequential subjects, was at the heart of the public relations program for quite a few years. Some firms developed it to an art, and could produce clippings in multiples of their competitors'. Soon, the competition for space was fought with clippings. Who got quoted more in *The Wall Street Journal*? Or *Business Week*? Or *The New York Times*?

But is this still the way to go? Is more still better?

Probably not. In the early days, when few firms were doing any sophisticated public relations, the few firms who could play the numbers game skillfully generated very high visibility. But ultimately, a few interesting facts emerged...

- Any name recognition generated by repeated mentions quickly faded when the mentions diminished for any reason. The staying power of name recognition built by these quickie mentions was very short-lived.

- As more sophisticated marketing techniques were brought into play, publicity became part of the overall program, and not necessarily the spearhead. While publicity is invaluable, the numbers game seems to contribute very little to the overall program.

- How do you convert those mentions, however many, into sales to prospective clients? True, reputation is important, and particularly the reputation for expertise. But it won't stand on its own, without moving people into a sales configuration.

- There got to be an easy tendency to rely on *volume* of mentions, rather than *quality* of mentions. This meant that a lot of effort was going into irrelevant publicity.

- As everybody learned the technique, everybody was getting into print, and nobody was distinguished. What had been exclusive became a mob scene, diluting the value of each mention for each firm. How do you compete effectively when everybody is doing the same thing, and saying the same thing?

An important element of publicity, in professional services marketing, is leadership. When you can't lead the pack, and are merely one of the pack, you're accomplishing nothing to enhance or establish your reputation.

No, more is not better. Better is better. Less publicity, but each placement more relevant to the firm's marketing needs. Fewer clippings, but each with more impact to the firm's reputation for expertise.

And relevance is better. Relevance to the overall marketing objective. Not publicity for publicity's sake, but for a reason.

{Chapter 29}

Getting To The Next Stage

*Sometimes Change Is Improvement –
Sometimes It Isn't. But It's Always Inevitable*

Speaking of change, as we have been in this book, in the several months it took to write it, and to choose from the hundreds – maybe thousands – of articles I've written over the years, a great deal has changed. And not just trivial stuff.

The movement to replace the hourly billing with value billing has accelerated. Firm mergers, consolidations, new boutique firms that bear little resemblance to the historical professional firms, new technology that makes obsolete technology that was itself only months old. It seems that observations (I don't make predictions) that I made decades ago about the need to go outside the firm for new sources of capital to finance growth have turned out to be accurate. New professional/marketers partnerships are springing up. Professional Services Marketing 3.0 is in full swing.

But there's an apparent paradox here. In the first half of the book I talk about change – in the second half I write about marketing practices that haven't changed in the decades since Bates turned the professional world upside down.

Well, not so paradoxical. In the world of carpentry, they build furniture and houses using the same tools that have been standard for centuries, even though those tools have been streamlined and redesigned and improved. Still the same tools. So it is with marketing.

The tools of marketing, with the exception of new media and new methods of communications, are still the same tools we used since at least the turn of the 21st Century. We just use them better. And we have several new media, which seem to be new tools, but aren't really. They're just different versions of the earliest means of communicating. We've gone from shouting out of caves, to carving messages in stone, to the printing press, radio, then television, and now the internet and the social media.

Yes, there are subtle differences. The news story is written differently today than it was 50 years or so ago. I've never fully subscribed to "the medium is the message," but I've written for years that the way the same message is delivered differs from one medium to the next. For the well trained and experienced marketer, that's no big deal.

Some interesting points. Change is inevitable. An old vaudeville line from the early part of the 20th century (but still valid) comes to mind. *Change your act or go back to the woods.* When the world in which you function changes – especially if there's a valid reason for the changes (like response to a changing economic environment) – you'd better change too. In professional services, tradition is good when you stick to the basic principles of your practice. But in a competitive environment, in which you compete by improving the way in which you function to better serve clients, you can still streamline and accommodate without destroying professionalism and integrity.

There's a good example of that in the automobile industry. First came the invention of the power driven vehicle, which threatened to replace the horse. Then came the mass produced car. In black. Then came the car in any color, plus innovations, like the electric starter, then came the flashy vehicle that automakers saw – and sold – as a sex symbol. All transportation, all a difference in the same thing, all evolution, the result of which was… *change.*

Another interesting point. In any process subject to evolutionary change, the future – always hard to predict – becomes even more so. Why? Because the stages in every evolutionary process are affected by random events that are unpredictable. This is a point I tried to make in earlier chapters. An example is Facebook. It could not have been invented had not the internet been invented. Who could have foreseen that this campus based program would have evolved as an international medium that's become integral to the business world? Who could have predicted LinkdIn, or even Twitter? Who could have predicted that the internet itself could have so changed communication to the point of diminishing newspapers so close to obsolescence?

I have always preached that the starting point of any writing should always begin with the question, *"What do I want readers to know, think, or feel after reading what I write?"* I'll make it easy for you.

I wrote this book to demonstrate that the world in which accountants and lawyers function has changed, and done so as a result of *Bates v. State Bar of Arizona,* which bred a new world of competition in the professions.

In order to compete in this new world, lawyers and accountants had to learn a new art form, called *marketing.*

This started an evolutionary process that is resulting in new forms of practicing law and accounting – new business models, new approaches to productivity to better serve clients, a new path that is resulting in change to a heretofore impenetrable professionalism.

Where once the professionals thought that marketing was ancillary to a practice – that marketers were from a different world – the new professional realizes that marketing is as integral to a practice as, say, cash management.

And now, professionals are learning how to participate more actively and effectively in the marketing process.

That's Professional Services Marketing 3.0.

Will there be 4.0? Probably. But that's up to the world to come. And as I said earlier in this book, prognostication is a mug's game.

What to do then?

Keep your eyes open. Watch it happen. Even help it happen. But recognize that ultimately, change will happen, whether you like it or not. Whether you help it or not, it will happen.

To be continued on *The Marcus Letter,* at www.marcusletter.com.

THE END